The Novels of Ngugi

A Study in the Theme of Exploitation

P. Padma

Prestige

an international publishing house

Published by
Prestige Books
3/28, East Patel Nagar
New Delhi 110 008
Ph. 9818755529
email: prestigebooks@gmail.com

ISBN: 81-7551-186-9

Printed at Chaman Offset Press, New Delhi 110 002

Contents

for

my parents

Smt. Neeraja

and

Sri P. Nagamuni Reddy

Rtd. Principal

Govt. Degree College, Kadapa.

Preface

Ngugi is an Anglophone African writer, who in his fictional works, gives a Kikuyu view of the bitter colonial war, thereby correcting healthily a white man's point of view of the Mau Mau Revolution. He, in his novels, exposes vividly the exploitation and all its pernicious ramifications first by the colonialists and later by neo-colonialists. His righteous indignation at the depraved human behaviour finds finest expression in his novels. In this book, an attempt has been made to study the theme of exploitation which is prominently and elaborately treated by Ngugi in his novels.

The book is divided into seven chapters. The first chapter is by way of a general introduction of the term exploitation and its nature. The second chapter is an introduction to Ngugi and the predisposing and precipitating influences on him in making him a committed writer. The third chapter offers a critical analysis of the exploitation of the Africans by the British on the basis of race and class in the colonial context. The fourth chapter is concerned with the exploitation of the Africans by their own fellow countrymen in colonial and neo-colonial imperialistic Kenya.

The fifth chapter is devoted to the African women who have been exploited in the colonial and the neo-colonial imperialistic Kenya, on the basis of race, class and gender. Protest and revolt which appear to be an answer for exploitation are taken up for discussion in the sixth chapter. The concluding chapter sums up the observations made in the preceding chapters and proceeds to attempt an evaluation of Ngugi's contribution to Commonwealth Literature.

I owe a deep sense of gratitude to Prof. T. Asoka Rani, S.P. Mahila University, Tirupati; Prof. P. Bayapa Reddy, S.K. University, Anantapur; Late Prof. C.D. Narasimhaiah, Director,

Dhvanyaloka, Mysore and Prof. V. Sasi Kumar, CIEFL, Hyderabad, for their timely help. I am thankful to my husband Dr. G. Satyanarayana Reddy for his encouragement.

I am thankful to the librarians of Sri Padmavathi Mahila Viswavidyalayam and Sri Venkateswara University libraries in Tirupati, C.I.E.F.L., University of Hyderabad and the Osmania University libraries in Hyderabad, the Andhra University library in Visakhapatnam and Jawaharlal Nehru University in Delhi for their generous help and kind co-operation in securing the relevant material.

P. PADMA

Chapter 1

Introduction

The erstwhile British colonies taught English language in their colonies but at a subsequent time the colonies broke the 'word' and freed their 'thought' in English. With the attainment of political freedom the language of the creative artists in the colonies acquired plasticity and received considerable attention in Britain. Nowadays, in countries like Nigeria, Ghana, Kenya, West Indies and in India, an important body of literature which is referred to as Commonwealth literature or postcolonial literature has come up. Viney Kirpal calls this third world literature by restricting it to Britain's former colonies.

> The term 'third world' refers to the non-aligned group of countries which do not belong to either the capitalist block or the communist block—the term is also being used broadly today to refer to the world's undeveloped countries, though quite a few of these countries are not non-aligned in their relationship with other countries.[1]

Bruce King calls this third world literature 'New Literatures in English.' C.D. Narasimhaiah has named it 'Commonwealth literature.' According to him, "Commonwealth found themselves for the first time at the giving end while the mother country began to be at the receiving end. And what it received was not gold, silver, diamond, jute, cotton, silk or spices but as they say, the things of the mind and the spirit. This one act alone gave a tremendous boost to the creative talent in commonwealth countries."[2] These lines of Narasimhaiah show that the writers from Commonwealth countries have produced a good body of literature that is being read with respect all over the world. Publishers like Oxford University Press, Heinemann, Chatto and Windus came forward to bring out books by Commonwealth writers.

The fiction from the third world countries has certain common features in it. The first factor that binds the fiction in the Third World is the native writers' awareness of present-day problems and the need to confront them. Colonisation stretching over many years in the third world countries has affected the natives' sensibility. The novelists from Africa attempt to depict to the reading public, the historical fact of colonisation and its far-reaching consequences on the present condition and status of his country. This attempt has developed into an urgent expression of the need to decolonise which Frantz Fanon has described as "the veritable creation of new men. . . . The thing, which has been colonised, becoming man during the same process by which it frees itself."[3] The native speaker, as Viney Kirpal rightly observes, "has articulated the necessity of regenerating the ex-colonial's dead spirit and the self-respect of shedding off the oppressive influence of colonisation and by depicting to the world at large, the native's very own national identity and achievement."[4]

Another factor that binds the novelists in the third world countries is the use of technique. Most of the novelists draw from their traditional literatures, beliefs, myths and oral forms. These writers have used English as a non-colonial language. The English language, as Sundaram rightly observes, "is so transparent that it can take on the tint of any country."[5] It has acquired much richness and variety through contact with the different cultural set-ups in which it has been used for creative literature. Most of the African writers do not wish to write English like the English and so they have tried out various experiments to give English the local touch.

Another factor that can be seen in this genre is that it is parochial and at the same time universal. It is parochial in that it describes a particular society's history, culture and politics. It is universal in that it portrays the ethos of a people in their society that becomes easily the ethos of the people in other societies. Of these Commonwealth countries, a considerable body of literature emanated from Africa.

It is necessary to discuss the background against which the African writers are writing. Africa, in the eyes of Europeans, has remained a dark continent since Prince Henry, the navigator in the fifteenth century, to the beginning of the twentieth century. In the eighteenth century, African people were considered to be in a 'state of nature' in perfect harmony with their environment. This has developed as a stereotype image, which is still very powerful. The lengthy description of a journey into Africa in a European novel at the end of the nineteenth century goes thus:

> Going up that river was like travelling back to the earliest beginnings of the world, when vegetation rioted on the earth and the big trees were kings. An empty stream, a great silence, an impenetrable forest. The air was warm, thick, heavy, sluggish. There was no joy in the brilliance of sunshine. . . . You lost your way on that river as you would in a desert. From everything you had known once.[6]

This is Africa of the European novel with impenetrable forests and trackless wilderness. Africa's landscape can be described only in paradox. It is a desert in which vegetation riots. Its beauty has no shape and meaning. This is Africa without Africans. It is in fact the 'heart of darkness.'

Conrad describes air breezing on the African continent as 'warm, thick, heavy and sluggish.' The African continent was the White man's grave till the end of the nineteenth century because of Malaria caused by the Anopheles mosquito. The Whites were not able to diagnose the cause for deaths there and blamed the air there. This remorse spread and delayed the exploration of the continent. It remained a 'Dark Continent' for a long time. African inhabitants appear a few miles further up the Congo on the next page of the novel, *Heart of Darkness*.

> We penetrated deeper and deeper into the heart of darkness. It was quiet there. At night sometimes the roll of drums behind the curtain of trees would run up the river and remain sustained faintly as if lowering in the air high over our heads, till the first break of day. . .
>
> We were wanderers on a prehistoric earth, on the earth that wore the aspect of an unknown planet. . . . But suddenly there would be a glimpse of rush walls, of peaked grass roofs, a burst of yells, a

> whirl of black limbs, a mass of hands clipping, of fact stamping, of bodies swaying, of eyes rolling, under the droop of heavy and motionless foliage . . . a black and incomprehensible frenzy. (41)

From this one gathers that Africans are not even living people, they are mere conglomerations of limbs, bodies and eyes. They are meaningless creatures in the forest. This image projected in literature was also projected in Tarzan films. Explorers, traders and missionaries had projected similar image. Africa reminded a trackless wilderness even after the discovery of extensive trade routes. Even after exploring elaborately the social institutions, its earlier image did not change. So most of the writers found in Africa what they had been conditioned to find. Literary image is only one of the many, which clusters around the idea of the 'Dark Continent.' It is the background around which most of the Africans are writing.

Regarding the debate about the human status of Africans, a similar image prevailed for a long time. Africans are called 'noble savages,' 'depraved cannibals,' 'children of nature' and so on. According to the Linnaean classification of humanity into the white, yellow, red and black races in the eighteenth century, the blacks were considered inferior to other races. Even in the nineteenth century, there was no change in the image projection of the Africans by the Europeans. Africans are placed below the white race in the ladder of Great Chain of Being. Darwin's 'Theory of Origin' stated that it was the fittest that survived and developed. According to this theory, Africans were backward because they were inferior. Even if any traces of past civilizations were found, it was argued that they could not be African. Various kinds of race and evolutionary theories joined forces to prove too strong the myth of 'the noble savage.'

To the north of the African continent lies the Great Sahara desert, which separates it from the European land. The remaining three sides of the continent are separated from other lands being surrounded by ocean. So this continent was difficult to explore. Nevertheless, several explorers and traders went round the continent and touched the land. The vast coastal line of African continent has been known since a long time. It was controlled for over four hundred years in trade by Arabs, Europeans and Asians. Till the eighteenth century, the Arabs and the Europeans established their castles on the long coastline and traded from there.

Early in the eleventh century itself trade routes stretched till northern Kenya. "Black slaves from East Africa had become known throughout the coastlands of the Indian Ocean."[7] The traders in tenth, eleventh and twelfth centuries gathered gold, ivory and above all slaves from Africa. All these they were able to collect through African middlemen. During this period, the interior of Africa remained virtually closed. "What happened economically in the thirteenth century . . . seems to have been mainly the intensification of the already established lines of commercial exploitation."[8] Even in the fifteenth century, throughout the Indian oceans the aims of Europeans were essentially commercial and maritime. The object of Europeans, especially Portuguese, was to supplant the pre-existing network of Arab sea-borne trade.

In the seventeenth and eighteenth centuries during which slave trade was in progress, Africans were in European economic terms 'noble savages.' In the beginning of the nineteenth century, British were building up a paramountcy of influence in the region through the single local authority. During this time, foreign merchants, concession-seekers and moneylenders were permitted to exploit the new economy. While palm oil and slaves were chief exporting commodities of West Africa, from East Africa, cloves and ivory became important items of exports. With the demand increasing, the British penetrated deep into the interiors of Kenya.

> Even if the export trade in slaves was decreasing, that in ivory was growing year after year. It was the search of ivory, rather than that for slaves, which took the coast men annually further and further into the interior; but slavery and its attendant evils were inseparable from the ivory trade.[9]

This slave trade has devastating effects upon African individuals and their societies at large. African middlemen, even chiefs, helped Europeans and Americans to increase their lucrative market. In return, Europeans supplied guns and other arms to the chiefs of clans. This created mistrust and warfare among the African tribes. The slave trade affected African economic conditions also. The European merchants tried to keep Africa closed to honest trade and other influences to prevent any interference with their supply of 'black cargos.' This isolation and devastation strengthened the myth of African 'inferiority' and hindered progression.

Later, in the colonial times, the actual status of slavery was made illegal. The new abolitionists called the Africans a fellow creature who might have fallen and therefore, they felt that there was a greater need for help. Even at this time their image did not change as 'primitives.'

European powers also wanted raw material to manufacture goods. They also wanted markets for their expanding economies. To possess African territories permanently, there grew competition among the European countries. In 1884-1885, the rules of the game were laid down by the Berlin Africa conference. According to the main rule laid down, a country should have occupied the territory before it claims it. The European colonies—Spain, France, Portugal, Italy and England—created artificial boundaries and changed the map of Africa, according to their needs.

Different European countries imposed different types of colonial rule. Whatever may be the difference, each country represented the bringing together of two radically different, often opposed, ways of looking at power, politics and economics. The major decisions of the European powers were still made in their motherlands. Naturally, they brought the metropolitan principles, systems from their lands and imposed them on the Africans with varying degrees of fiction. In 1922, Lord Lugard in "The Dual Mandate" expounded the system of indirect rule. At that time, administrators were of the opinion that hierarchical African societies could be fitted more neatly into the colonial system. Later it was found too late that the assimilation of feudal chiefdoms could not be incorporated easily into a modern state. As a result of the meeting of two different power structures, a variety of problems and misunderstandings arose.

European rationalisation extended in other fields. Attempts were made to establish African people in fixed communities with rights to their land. The British sought to regulate African courts also. This restricted the traditional flexibility of African societies. The colonial system aimed at controlling African societies more effectively.

European missionaries worked as effective intermediaries between two cultures. They took it as the White man's burden to 'civilize' the 'uncivilized people.' Europeans condemned the black man's civilization and dismissed any trace of past civilization. They made attempts to reform the African rituals. As the traditional values were destroyed, missionaries supplied answers to the new questions that were being asked. To this end, they started missionary schools to educate the 'primitive.' Whatever was unintelligible and incomprehensive was labelled as meaningless and absurd. They projected their own fears and insecurity and condemned the native's religion. As a result, there was an over-all attempt to put on a white mask to cover the black face. Like the administrators, the missionaries also had occupational needs to consolidate the image of savage Africa. The native's failure to respond to alien culture and values was painted as another evidence of its inferiority.

In introduction to *An Anthology of Essays on African Literature*, Ernest N. Emenyou says, "Oral literature which is the foundation of modern African literature is as old as man in Africa."[10]

Piozinimu, a Ugandan linguist and literary critic coined the term "orature" to denote stories, poems, plays etc., which are transmitted orally. Oral literature is in a well-documented form now. African fiction draws heavily on its oral literature.

Now, a number of African writers are writing in English and French. African literature has drawn much attention from different parts of the world. Wole Soyinka (1986) and Nadine Gordimer (1991) were awarded the Nobel Prize for literature. Amos Tutuola, Ayi Kwi Armah, Cyprian Ekwensi, Wole Soyinka, Chinua Achebe, Ngugi wa Thiong'o are the most popular Anglophone novelists. Sembene Ousmana, Ferdinand Oyonyo and Camara Laye are popular writers of Francophone fiction. Peter Abrahams, Alex La Guma, Alam Patar, Nadine Gordimer and Richard Reve are well-known South African novelists. Flora Nwapa, Buchi Amecheta, Ama Ata Aidoo, Bessie Head are some of the famous women writers from Africa.

Just as any other art of Africa, literature also has functional value in African society. Most of the African writers reject the theory of art for art's sake. Achebe says, "Art for Art's sake is just another piece of deodorized dog-shit. . . . Art is and was always in the service of man."[11]

African writers are in the mainstream of society. The role of such African writer is juxtaposed with the alienated image of his European counterpart away from their roots and also from their tradition.

African government is a pluralistic government. It is not a unitary system. It is not rigid and codified but in continual process of examination and change. The flexibility of its government is lost with the imposition of European government. Africans became puppets in the hands of the white puppeteers. After the white masters left the colonies in Africa, they were in most cases succeeded by the Black puppeteers. Naturally, the writers in Africa particularly in the nineteen sixties attempted to voice their reaction, thoughts and grudge on the nature of change brought over in their societies by the imperialistic powers. They not only voiced their protest but also shattered the good old African myth about the much-published inferiority of the African culture and civilization in pre-colonial days. Chinua Achebe says:

> I would be quite satisfied if my novels (especially, the ones I set in the past) did no more than teach my readers that their past—with all its imperfections—was not one long night of savagery from which the first Europeans acting on God's behalf delivered them.[12]

The creative writers from Africa never hesitated to preserve their myths, legends and superstitions prevalent in their societies. They in a way freed themselves from the blind limitations of white man's values. They tried to preserve self-respect and dignity of human beings. They interpreted the past in their own way and analyzed the change from their particular point of view. They did not hesitate to express their disillusionment at the realisation that their hopes for recovery after independence were being foiled by the neo-colonial forces. They became so confident that they felt that they could continue their struggle at present. They aimed at complete freedom from all impositions and bondages in social, political or cultural realms. Thus creative literature in English written in Africa has an impact of the colonial experience on the native's consciousness. Secondly, it records "the native writer's increasing awareness of the peculiar present-day problems . . . and his growing concern with the need to confront them."[13]

Colonisation stretching over a long period in Africa introduced new modes of production, started a system of liberal education that has helped the native to question traditional authoritarian and superstitious modes of thought. It also introduced liberal religion in Africa. After attaining freedom, they did not make strides on the economic and social front as they have failed to confront the problems of poverty, unemployment, overpopulation, hunger, illiteracy and disease. On the political front the fate of the common man never changed as the local leadership continuously exploited him. The colonisation affected the native character and confidence.

The creative writer in Africa understands the subversive impact that colonisation has had on the colonial's consciousness. His attempt therefore has been constantly to depict to the reading public, the historical fact of colonisation and its far-reaching consequences on the present conditions and the status of his country. So he feels that there is a desperate need 'to decolonise the thing which has been colonized.'

The native speaker has articulated the necessity of regenerating the ex-colonials, dead spirit and self-respect of shutting of the oppressive influence of colonisation and by depicting to the world at large, the natives' own national identity and achievements.

The creative writers in Africa deeply feel that the purpose of writing is to teach and educate. According to them this can be done in two ways: first by asserting the beauty and dignity of his own culture, and secondly, by educating the masses in the new direction the country must take as a mature independent nation. In other words, these writers are mostly committed to these ideals and they waged a war against exploitation. It is pertinent at this point to note the nature and meaning of the term 'exploitation.'

The word 'Exploitation,' broadly speaking, implies unfair utilisation of a person or a community for one's own selfish ends. The victim of exploitation is made to suffer irretrievably. There are myriad ways in which the exploited are affected socially, economically, psychologically and even politically. A committed writer takes a clear stand against the exploiters. A committed writer is one who, through his work, is dedicated to the advocacy of certain beliefs and programmes, especially those which are political or ideological and in aid of social reform. He keeps in mind the exploited and comes out with his commitment that arises from the sense of moral fervour and righteousness. He has the willingness to work for a well-defined ideology aimed at reform. As William Horosz says:

> Commitment is an awareness, an attitude, a clear and feelingful recognition of being fully present in the moment, making the choice of the moment and standing by the consequences of these choices whether anticipated or not.[14]

Creative artists do not live in a vacuum. They are sensitive to the world around them more acutely than others. So their works reflect the deepest mood of their times. In a way, they are shaped by their age and they mould their age too. In an epoch of intense social transformation, political, economic and social forces influence upon the artists' responses to these forces.

The forces of exploitation may differ in each sphere. Certain writers align themselves very much with the economic, social and political issues of the age and attack the exploiters boldly by violently disapproving and protesting against the exploiters. The exposures of the evil practices of the exploiters and the registering of their protest have become major functions of literature in some societies. In other words, the writer commits himself to an ideology or an institution. As long as the artist is concerned with aesthetic commitment, it does not pose any problem to him. The problem arises when he is committed to values or actions extrinsic to the immediate concerns of his art. In other words, if he is committed to certain social objectives, he is invariably involved with considerations of means of realising them. For example, if a writer feels that the individuals of a society have become a prey to the exploitation of the landlord, he without any favour or fear, may record the exploiter's situation, question the landlord and also stir similar exploited ones to wage a war against the landlord. In the words of Gerald Rabkin, "The artist is expected to involve himself with social questions to immerse himself in the milieu of which he is an integral part."[15]

A socially committed writer enquires into the drawbacks of society leading to the sincere understanding of the problem. Secondly, he considers and suggests the possible remedial measures for the ills in society. Thirdly, he indicates the methods of implementing the solution.

A committed writer makes a ruthless scrutiny of the social evils, which are repugnant to him and to his people. He shouts and for the visually impaired, he draws large and startling figures. He shows the means to correct the distortions and to remedy the situation by calling attention to the fatal eventuality of frenzied action and the equally fatal consequences of apathy. Clifford Odets and Auden in the U.S., Mulk Raj Anand and Harindranath Chattopadhyaya in India, Arnold Wesker in England, Ngugi in Kenya are some of the creative artists who never hesitated to invite others to listen to them and subjected their works to the scrutiny of their people. Their art is committed to the people, to revolution and transformation. It contributes to revolutionary change and it preserves everything that is good for humanity. In other words, by recording the ills in society, it remains on the side of the oppressed.

In the early nineteenth century, Karl Marx, the exponent of Marxist theory, defined exploitation in capitalist terms. But when Ngugi is asked how he views the observation that he has leftist inclination, he says:

> I believe in a national economy free from any foreign domination or free from imperialist control. These are my fairly simple beliefs and what labels are put on them is really the business whoever fixing the labels on these simple beliefs.[16]

Thus, he expresses his opinion in an interview after Kenya got independence. Exploitation is one of the besetting evils inhibiting man from the times immemorial in some way or the other. It has been more so during the British hegemony. This resulted in untold misery to the Africans. Ironically, even after the attainment of the freedom from the colonists the canker of exploitation continues to bedevil the lives of large sections of Kenyans by their own countrymen. Ngugi observes exploitation as a human aberration and his righteous indignation at this depraved human behaviour finds finest expression in his novels. In this book, an attempt has been made to study the theme of exploitation which is prominently and elaborately treated by Ngugi wa Thiong'o.

NOTES

1. Viney Kirpal, "The Third World Fiction," *Recent Commonwealth Literature* (New Delhi: Prestige, 1989) p. 10.
2. C.D. Narasimhaiah, ed., "Introduction," *Commonwealth Literature* (New Delhi: Oxford University Press, 1976), p. 6.
3. Frantz Fanon, *The Wretched of the Earth* (London: Macgibben and Ree, 1965), pp. 29-30.
4. Kirpal, p. 13.
5. P.S. Sundaram, *R.K. Narayan* (New Delhi: Arnold Heinemann, 1973), p. 130.
6. Joseph Conrad, *Heart of Darkness* (Bombay: Orient Longman, 1996), p. 39.
7. Roland Oliver and J.D. Fage. "North-East and East Africa in Medieval and Early Modern Times," *A Short History of Africa* (England: Penguin, 1975), p. 98.
8. *Ibid.*, p. 100.

9. *Ibid.*, p. 179.
10. Ernest Ngugi Emenyonu, *African Literature Comes of Age*, ed. Ernest Emenyonu and C.D. Narasimhaiah (Mysore: Dhvanyaloka Publications, 1988), p. v.
11. Chinua Achebe, *Morning Yet on Creation Day* (London: Heinemann, 1975), p. 19.
12. Chinua Achebe, "The Role of Writer in a New Nation," *Nigeria Magazine* (Lagos), Vol. 81 (1964), p. 157.
13. Kirpal, p. 11.
14. William Horosz, *The Crisis of Responsibility: Man as the Source of Accountability* (Horman: University of Oklahoma Press, 1975), p. 248.
15. Gerald Rabkin, *Drama and Commitment* (Bloomington: Indiana University Press, 1964), p. 14.
16. "People have right to know," Interview by Magina with m(2UNgugi wa Thiong'o, *African Report*, No. 9 (Feb. 1979), p. 90.

Chapter 2

Ngugi wa Thiong'o: Predisposing and Precipitating Influences

Ngugi was born at Kamarithu, Limuru, near Nairobi on 5 January 1938. It was the period when the coloniser established in the so-called "white highlands in the heart of Gikuyu country."[1] The white settlers in Kenya took the most fertile land from a group whose population was increasing and dependent on land and agriculture for its survival. The large armies of landless men were forced to sell their labour to white farmers on their own ancestral lands, which had been confiscated by law. Ngugi's father also lost his land and became 'ahoi' working on the lands owned by others. Ngugi was brought up in an unsafe environment and discomfiture. Since his childhood, he developed profoundly disturbing psychological nuances that later became moving spirit behind his works.

Ngugi's education also has something to do with the kind of writer he became later. He was admitted in Gikuyu independent school, Kamundura, Limura. The Gikuyu independent schools were founded and operated by Gikuyu people who had rebelled against the missionary influence. Their aim was to provide education of a kind appropriate to the African setting. Later he joined an Alliance High School. In an interview, he says:

> As I see them in their historical role, they have been the forerunners of colonist. . . . The colonial administration. As an African, he could be taken in Cambridge but not on the basis of merit, more of a gesture, of course, we protested, but inwardly we believed it and unconsciously had a high regard for the white boys.[2]

After secondary school, he joined Makerere University College, Kampala, in 1959 where he remained until 1964. It was the oldest of the University Colleges of East Africa. He sees university education in East Africa at that time as an extension of colonial education in the missionary schools. In his own words:

> You must see universities in Africa in their colonialist missionary setting. They did not want you to question things or compare western institutions with other systems. For instance those who studied Political Science heard of Karl Marx only as an incidental rather eccentric figure. You would never have thought that he was one of the people whose doctrine has influenced two thirds of the world.[3]

These lines show the colonial education policy in Africa that was never liked by Ngugi.

During his college days, Ngugi had an opportunity of reading the works of D.H. Lawrence and Conrad who, at a later date, shaped him as a creative artist. One can see Ngugi having D.H. Lawrence as a literary model. In an interview with Denis Duerden, he says, "I discover D.H. Lawrence and his way of entering into the spirit of things influenced me quite a lot."[4]

It was from Lawrence that he learned to enter into the soul of people and of the land of the countryside, of things like plants of the atmosphere. He continues to say thus: "When I am reading D.H. Lawrence, I feel the spirituality of things very near me as if I am touching the very spirit of things."[5]

Conrad also appealed to him much. The African writer and Joseph Conrad share the same world. Both have lived a world dominated by capitalism, imperialism and colonialism. G.D. Killam, in the words of Peter Nazareth a friend and fellow student at Makarere, tells: "Ngugi learnt a good deal of technique from contemplation of Conrad's writing, a technique which would sustain the affinity of sensibility."[6]

One can see Conradian echoes in Ngugi's work, particularly in his *A Grain of Wheat*. The accumulated guilt of the colonised, a social fact which partly explains the echoes of Conrad, the exile writing in a foreign tongue stirred his intellect. In 1974, Ngugi described his interest in Conrad as centring on his concern with the morality of action. In his words,

> Reading Conrad one feels struck by man's capacity for bearing suffering but much more than this, he questions what appears on the surface. He questions what I would call the morality of action . . . this kind of questioning has impressed me a lot because with Conrad, I have felt, I have come in contact with other language whose questioning to me is much more important than the answers he gives.[7]

The way society develops under colonialism draws its members into the position of social isolation and consequent moral doubt which Conrad, exiled for life from his Polish home, has also made the central preoccupation of his writing. Like Conrad, Ngugi recorded the social isolation and moral doubt in his works.

Ngugi met Jonathan Kariara, editor of *Pen Point*, a journal at the centre of the creative efforts on Makarere hill. During his student days at Makerere College, there was a gathering of African writers where writers like Achebe, Soyinka and J.P. Clark participated. In fact, they tried to formulate a definition of African literature and African ethos. This has formed a deep impression on Ngugi and touched his mental proclivities and sharpened his assertions about the role of a writer.

After graduating from Makerere College in 1964, he worked for a while on Nairobi's *Daily Nation* for which he contributed a column entitled "As I Seek." This apprenticeship in journalism made him understand the social, economic and political conditions of Kenya. Moreover, he granted several interviews and progressively gave expression to a pattern of thought that steadily grew and deepened in response to the changing contemporary social and political environment.

After graduation, Ngugi went to Leeds for higher studies. During his stay in England, he met many young radicals notably in the group led by Allan Haunt as well at forthright literary discussions in the house of Arnold Kettle. At the University of Leeds, he studied for Masters Degree in English. He expressed "his skepticism about higher degrees as elitist symbols from this time."[8]

Ngugi went back to East Africa and saw some changes during the 'heady years there.' The individual countries—Tanganyika, Uganda, Zanzibar and Kenya—though attained independence, remained as the members of a closely-knit East African community of Nations, for a time sharing common transportation and communication system and a common currency. Unity was more than a slogan to the then nationalist politicians who had led their areas of the world of a self-rule. Ngugi ventured to discuss social and political problems boldly in some of the leading journals of the country.

Ngugi joined English department as a lecturer at the University College in Nairobi where he served for a year and half. When there was a student strike in January 1969, he resigned his post on 27 January in protest against the dictatorial attitude of the university administration towards the student body during and after the strike. He along with Tabai Lo Liyong and Henry Vouor-Anyumba, formulated the proposal for the abolition of English department and for starting a department of African literature and languages in that university. Ngugi summed up along with his friends the recommendation thus:

> For any group it is better to study representative works, which mirror their society, rather than to study a few isolated classics either of their own or of a foreign culture. . . . We went to establish the centrality of Africa in the department. This is justifiable on various grounds, the most important one being that education is a means of knowledge about ourselves. . . . The dominant object in that perspective is African literature, the major branch of African culture.[9]

After the resignation from the University College in Nairobi, Ngugi went to North-Western University, U.S.A. where he conducted research and also devoted considerable time to creative writing. During his stay in U.S.A., he witnessed many literary trends which shaped him later as a writer. In 1970, he went back to Kenya and took up a second appointment in the literature department at the University of Nairobi. He assumed the headship in 1972.

Frantz Fanon exercised great influence on Ngugi who read Fanon's *The Wretched of the Earth* and drew thoughts from it.

He was impressed by Fanon's analysis of colonialism in Africa. Fanon felt that the imperialist powers would not hand over independence and that independence could only be attained through violence, for Europe had laid hand on Africa and would not go unless the fingers were hacked off. To him, it was only violence, revolutionary violence organised and carried out by the masses that can succeed in winning independence. Like Frantz Fanon, Ngugi also thought that only by struggle and revolution the Kenyans would get back their land. In fact, in his novels, he describes the attempts made by the Kenyans to get back their lands beginning with Waiyaki and Harry Khuku.

Fanon's another book *Black Skin, White Masks* describes the socio-economic causes within the context of armed revolution. He attributed the myth of colour as the main cause of racist oppression. He saw that colonialism was based on technological power. So he wanted to prevent man from feeling a stranger in his own environment. It was the environment that has to be changed. He saw how man had to live in his conscience with the recollection of the consequence of his action. Peter Nazareth rightly traces the psychological situation of people in *A Grain of Wheat*. Like Fanon, Ngugi feels that the sacred soul must regain its hold.

Jomo Kenyatta also influenced Ngugi's thought markedly. In fact, it was Kenyatta who tried to present, in his *Facing Mount Kenya*, the Gikuyu way of life with the greatest amount of sympathy and understanding. He shared a widespread human tendency to idealise the past. The book with its nostalgic views of Gikuyu culture was not an atavistic call for regression to tribal tradition. Ngugi made it clear that he admired Kenyatta as an African writer who would, for a long time, remain in the forefront of the intellectuals who tried to interpret Gikuyu culture. He admired and applauded Kenyatta, an anthropologist and politician. In *Facing Mount Kenya*, Kenyatta says:

> A culture has no meaning apart from the social organization of life on which it is built. When the European comes to the Gikuyu country and robs the people of their land, he is taking away not

> only their livelihood but the material symbol that holds family and tribe together.[10]

This deep-felt conviction of Kenyatta pervades much of the writings of Ngugi.

As a writer from the third world, Ngugi never hesitated to read West Indian literature and in fact he found it to be very interesting. He says:

> The West Indies is a mixed community and also the literature is just emerging and there would be interesting parallels and contrasts and comparisons between this emergent West Indian literature and the new literature from Africa.[11]

He was enthralled by reading some of the writings of Lamming and Naipaul. Rightly does he say thus:

> I was overwhelmed by George Lamming, I read him uncritically—almost everything he wrote, uncritically—from cover to cover. He really overwhelmed me.[12]

Besides Lamming, he read all the works of Naipaul. Much of Naipaul's imagination has gone into the works of Ngugi. Like Lamming and Naipaul, his work is set in the social situation prevailing during his times.

Peter Abrahams also influenced to certain extent the writings of Ngugi. He says about Peter Abrahams:

> When I went to Makerere, 1959, I was very much taken up with Peter Abrahams. I found his stories very moving and I tried to read as many novels as I could.[13]

Though Abraham's style did not appeal to him, he got impressed with the subject matter of his novels and felt that he should also stir his people with his writing. Particularly *Song of the City*, *Mine Boys* and the *Path of Thunder* by Peter Abrahams influenced him.

The Mau Mau movement which took place in Kenya between October 1952 and October 1953 was an armed peasant revolt aimed at reclaiming land given to white farmers by the English Government. It developed into guerilla warfare in the dense jungle areas in the Abodare mountains and around Mount Kenya just north of Nairobi. Gikuyu, Embu, Meru and Masai tribesmen were living and fighting in the forest. At the height of the fighting fifteen thousand men mostly Gikuyu died. Some felt "Mau Mau was not primarily a political movement but an atavistic return to a state of savagery."[14]

This movement influenced many Kenyans and directed a line of thought in their writings. The young Ngugi never appreciated Majdolany's description of the Gikuyu people as primitive and akin to Stone Age. In his *Homecoming*, he assets thus:

> To most Africans Mau Mau in fact, was a heroic and glorious aspect of the mainstream of African nationalism. . . . Mau Mau violence was anti injustice; while violence was to thwart the cause of justice. (27-28)

As a creative artist, Ngugi earnestly felt that he should respect the Mau Mau revolution and the history of the people. His first three novels sincerely set out to disapprove of the specific charges made by the colonialist historians to restore Gikuyu values, and to redeem the Mau Mau movement. He felt that Mau Mau was a political movement with legitimate aims and not cruel murderers. Like Waiyaki in *The River Between*, he realized:

> All at once he felt more forcefully than he has felt before that shame of people's land being taken away, the shame of being forced to work on those same lands, the humiliation of paying taxes for the government that you knew nothing about. . . . Now he knew what he would preach if he never got another chance . . . education for unity. Unity for political freedom. (RB, 142-43)

The above lines show how Mau Mau revolution exercised the young Ngugi. In fact, his works read as revolutionary manuals rousing national consciousness and they are embedded in his early agonizing anger and his deep commitment to his nation.

The literary career of Ngugi may conveniently be divided into two periods—the early period ranging from 1962 to 1967 and the later period ranging from 1968 to 1981. Since 1981, he has been displaying his talent in his native Gikuyu. Perhaps, he thought that he would reach most of the people in the country if he did it in Gikuyu.

Ngugi began his literary career during his student days at Makerere College, where he contributed his short story entitled "The Fig Tree" to *Pen Point*, a literary magazine, published by the University English department. His next short story "The Wind" was published three months later in *Pen Point*. From this modest beginning he went on composing some more short stories, besides the first draft of a novel called *The Black Messiah* (later entitled *The River Between*). As one of his compeers at Makerere rightly observes:

> This young writer makes his stories deal with the day-to-day life in the villages—problems caused by drought, the village medicine man versus an African priest, the tension between the old and the new ways of life and so on. His success indicates that the secret lies in dealing with reality—with or without an African background.[15]

These lines show his concern for the problems of the people in the society around him. Most of his early short stories were reprinted in *Secret Lives and Other Stories*.

Besides his short stories, the young Ngugi evinced interest in journalism, thereby rousing the consciousness of his people. Between May 1961 and August 1964, he wrote nearly eighty pieces for the Nairobi press contributing to the *Sunday Post*. He also prepared a fairly regular column for *Sunday Nation* and worked as a full-time junior reporter and editorial commentator for the *Daily Nation* in the months between his graduation from Makarere and his departure for postgraduate studies at Leeds University in England. The features and articles, besides exhibiting his protest, captured "the intricacies of human situation with compassion and understanding and feeling the throb of life in the nation."[16]

Ngugi during the early period felt that one of the best ways of stimulating greater practical contribution by African to the national culture was through theatre. He applauded the efforts of amateur theatre groups whose productions he has seen in Nairobi and Kampala and tried to encourage the formation of such theatre groups. He even reviewed a production of *The Lion and the Jewel* by Wole Soyinka. His own interest led him to write a play *The Black Hermit*, which was produced by the Uganda National Theatre in November 1962. The notices of the play brought public attention to him for the first time.

In his preface to *The Black Hermit*, Ngugi comes out with the very purpose of writing of this play:

> I thought then that tribalism was the biggest problem besetting the new East African countries. I along with my fellow undergraduates had faith in the postcolonial governments. We thought they genuinely wanted to involve the message in the work of reconstruction. After all, weren't the leaders themselves sons and daughters of peasants and workers? All the people had to do was to co-operate. All we had to do was to expose and root out the cankerous efforts of tribalism, racialism and religious factions.[17]

Rightly does this work enquire into "the betrayal of the legitimate aspirations of peasantry."[18]

Whitman, a great nineteenth century poet of America stirred the imagination of quite a few creative writers in the world. In paying a tribute to Whitman, Rabindranath Tagore once said, "Whitman is the highest name. . . . He has seen deeply and knows humanity. He gives me pictures—pictures!"[19] Ngugi also is impressed by his 'humanity' and 'pictures.' Whitman's poem "On the Beach at Night" dramatizes his happy confident mood in 1871. The protagonist in the poem encourages the child not to weep and also not to entertain any anxiety and fear. The father says:

> Weep not, child
> Weep not, my darling
> With these kisses, let me remove your tears,
> The ravening clouds shall not be victorious,
> They shall not long possess the sky.[20]

The epigraph of Ngugi's novel *Weep Not, Child* is from Whitman's poem, which provides the necessary backdrop to the novel. Like the child in Whitman's poem, the Gikuyu people are in the grip of fear. They feel that their land has been taken away by the colonizers. They are of the opinion that the land is the source of life to them.

Jomo Kenyatta in his *Facing Mount Kenya* describes the same belief thus:

> Communion with the ancestral spirit is perpetuated through contact with the soil in which the ancestors of the tribe lie buried. The Gikuyu considers the Earth, the mother of the tribe for the reasons that the mother bears her burden for about eight or nine moons while the child is in her womb and then for a short period of suckling. But it is the soil that feeds the child through a lifetime . . . and again after death it is the soil that nourishes the spirit of the tribe for a futurity. Thus the Earth is the most sacred thing above all that dwells in or on it. (21)

Among the Gikuyu the soil is especially honoured and everlasting oath is to swear by the earth. The systematic alienation of the land by the British and also the brutal exploitation at the hands of the British are artistically expressed in Ngugi's novel *Weep Not, Child.*

Ngotho, the protagonist, works on land, once the ancestral land of his forebears is now owned by Howlands, the white settler. He lives on the same land, but now owned by Jacobo, a black chief. Ngotho acquiesces to his circumstances because he is confident of the prophecy of the Gikuyu sage Mugo wa Kibiro, that the land will be returned to its rightful owners. This small village of Ngotho is a microcosm of Kenya at the time of the emergency at the initial stages. The principal characters, Ngotho, Howlands, Boro, Jacobo, Njoroge represent various points of view. Certain scenes in the novel have a symbolic significance. The most notable of these is the one relating to Howlands who threatens to castrate Njoroge as he has done to his father Ngotho. It is suggestive of the desire of Europeans to deprive the Africans of their rights and manhood. In this first published novel, Ngugi depicts graphically the exploitation of the Africans at the hands of the Europeans.

Ngugi's next published work *The River Between* appeared in 1965. Ngugi also discusses a feudal class of people in the grip of superior power and in the sway of new ideas. Ngugi discusses the exploitation of the tribes by the Europeans. He also describes the theme of exploitation of one tribe by the other. He earnestly describes a traditional society that reacts to change as alien ideas are imposed on indigenous culture. There are characters that express various points of view and various types of exploitation. In a way, he dwells upon the theme of exploitation in the realms of religion, politics and social structure.

The two villages, which *The River Between* describes—Kameno and Mykuyu—are separated by River Honia symbolising life. They were in relative harmony before they were affected by the alien religion and colonial politics. There is discussion on Christianity that was introduced recently. Traditional religion and Christianity, the clashes between the two tribes and the scheming nature of reformers and statesmen etc., find place in the novel. The leadership is very much distanced from the throng. In the words of David Cook,

> The novel depicts a situation in which a properly unified programme for defending the integrity of indigenous society is dangerously split between rival polity. Education and political activism, instead of being partners become antagonist.[21]

A Grain of Wheat is another published novel that concerns itself with the Mau Mau independence war leading to the Kenyan independence. The epigraph from "Corinthians," runs thus:

> Thou fool, that which thou sowest is not quickened, except it die. And that which thou sowest, thou sowest not that body, that shall be, but bare grain, it may chance of wheat, or of some other grain.[22]

Here, Saint Paul answers the Corinthians who have misgiving about the resurrection of the mortal body and about the Second Coming.

> The passage taken together with the other forms a continuum, which asserts that sacrifice will prompt change and draws attention to the reasons for the sacrifice. This in turn will draw attention to the possibility of achieving the New Jerusalem according to the vision of Saint John, the divine.[23]

This passage from the Bible has an association with the situation in Kenya in which sacrifices are called for and in which assurance of the legitimacy of the sacrifices made is needed. The paradox of the death that prompts new life to the Second Coming and to the possibility of a New Heaven and a New Earth is associated with in the novel with Mugo-Wa-Kibero, Waiyaki and Harry Thiku. Kihika is the most recent edition to the list of legendary names. And in their way, each of the characters left alive after the struggles achieves a new birth on 'Uhuru' day.

Ngugi shows us the predominance of the people of Kenya and lays interest in victims of the emergency. There are reports of Kihika's activities—especially of the incident, which earned him a place among the martyrs of the land by killing of D.O. Robson. But Kihika reports this to Mugo. What it was like to be with the forest fighters is always reported. We never travel into the bush to be with them. Thus Ngugi records and also pays tribute to the actions of the freedom fighters of the independent movement in Kenya in this novel. There is also a legitimate quest on his part for a return of the land by the exploiters to the people of Kenya, the exploited.

Ngugi's next work *Short African Plays* appeared in 1972. *The Rebels* reiterates the theme of *The Black Hermit*. Various characters in the play reject the new ways put forth by the government. Charles, husband of Mary, cries out thus:

> It is doing of all of us who forget that Africa is one and it is the name of one black race now bowed down by years of white misery and misshapen education.[24]

These lines show the theme of rejection of the government policies. His next play, *The Wound in the Heart*, deals with Ruhiu's triumph and anger. The protagonist expresses his anger against white domination and the detention of the Africans by the Europeans. Even *This Time Tomorrow* dwells upon the bitterness of 'Uhuru' caused by the earners of the new African rulers who imitate the recently deposed white ones. Thus even his *Short African Plays* is based on Ngugi's interest in the theme of exploitation.

Secret Lives is a collection of short stories. In the preface to *Secret Lives*, Ngugi observes that the stories are from his creative autobiography and that they touch on the ideas and moods that affected him and his writings.

The first three stories that constitute part I titled "Mothers and Children" tell of the relations between mothers and children. The first two stories "Mugomo" and "And the Rain Came Down" tell of childless women subjected to humiliation in the society. "Gone with the Drought" tells of a severe drought that had affected the land and of the young narrator's concern for an old woman of the village who was thought by most of the villagers to be mad.

Part II entitled, "Fighters and Martyrs" treats of events in the period defined by the coming of the White man through his departure from Kenya. He focuses his attention on the secret lives of the characters in circumstances that produce a good deal of tension.

Part III entitled, "Secret Lives" shows the consequences of historical process initiated by the introduction of modern values and methods in education, religion and business. In *Secret Lives* "Ngugi is concerned with the new Africa with the quantity of life in the here and now."[25]

His next book, *The Homecoming*, a collection of his essays primarily on society and literature, appeared in 1972. According to Ngugi these essays form part of the fictional world of the first three novels. In this work, he expresses his beliefs and ideas and his commitment to the goal of African revolution. He reveals to us the very purpose of writing his essays:

> In a novel, the writer is totally immersed in a world of imagination that is other than his conscious self. At his most intense and creative the writer is transformed. He is poked. He becomes a medium. In the essay the writer can be more direct, didactic, polemical or he can merely state his beliefs and faith. . . . The writer is thus forced either by the public or by the needs of his craft to define his beliefs, his attitudes and outlook in the more argumentative form of the essay. (xv)

Through essays in *Homecoming*, Ngugi makes a fervent plea for a prime of place for the African studies. In an article "The Writer and his Past," he comes out with his deep-felt convictions:

> I want to talk about the past as a way of talking about the present. . . . I want to argue that what has been . . . the evolution of human culture through the ages, society in motion through time and space—it is a great import to the writer. For what has been, specially, for the vast majority of submerged exploited masses in Africa, Asia and Black America is intimately bound up with what might be our vision of the future, of diverse possibilities of life and human potential, our roots in our experience of the past. (16)

These lines throw light on his theory of history that has a strong influence on the underlying thematic purposes of his creative writing.

Next appeared *The Trial of Dedan Kimathi*, a play written by Ngugi and his friend Micere Githae Mugo. This play attempts to restore the character of Kimathi to his legitimate place in the history of Kenya. Dedan Kimathi fought for the liberation of the Kenyan people from foreign domination and oppression. He did not achieve this liberation in his lifetime. But he continued his struggle till his dcath. Ngugi and his colleague Micere Githae Mugo have collaborated in writing a play with a specific purpose. This is primarily intended to sing the glory of Kimathi and his brothers Koaitalel and Me Kitilili who played their role in revolution. In the preface, the authors write:

> We agreed that the most important thing was for us to reconstruct imaginatively our history envisioning the world of Mau Mau and Kimathi in terms of the peasants and workers' struggle before and after constitutional independence. The play is not a reproduction of the farcical 'trial' at Ned. It is rather an imaginative reconstruction and interpretation of the collective will of the Kenyan peasants and workers in their refusal to break under sixty years of colonial torture and ruthless oppression by the British ruling classes and their continued determination to resist exploitation, oppression and new forms of enslavement.[26]

This play powerfully connects the struggle of the Kenyan people with other revolutionary people. It ends with an exhortation to the working classes and peasants to become a revolutionary force thereby attacking the exploiters.

Ngugi's next novel, *Petals of Blood*, has rightly got a maxim from Walt Whitman who earnestly felt that democracy was a true leveller. The title of the novel is from Derek Walcott's poem, "The Swamp." In his *Castaway Poems*, Derek Walcott makes use of the myth of Robinson Crusoe who robs the rich and helps the poor. The lines from Walcott's poem "The Swamp" run thus:

> Fearful, original, sinuosities! Each mangrove sapling
> Serpent like, its roots obscene
> As a six-fingered hand,
>
> conceals within its clutch the mossbacked toad,
> Toadstools, the potent ginger-lily,
> Petals of blood,
>
> The speckled vulva of the tiger-orchid
> Outlandish Phalloi
> Haunting the travellers of its one road.[27]

The poet here feels that a huge tree prevents little flowers from reaching out into the light. It is akin to the social system of capitalism and imperialism that stifle life. In this novel, Ngugi doesn't hesitate to exhibit varied kind of exploitation particularly in the realms of education, religion and agriculture. He has added an artistic representation of the betrayal of the independence movement and the need for the creation of a cultural liberation struggle fostered by the peasants and workers. In one of the interviews, he says:

> In a nutshell, I would say that I believe our national economy reflected in our culture should be able to develop freely but that Kenyan wealth should feed, clothe and shelter Kenyans.[28]

The novelist is on the side of the peasants and workers. The four parts of the novel take us back to 1896 when the exploitation of Kenyans by Europeans began and in some passages to the prehistorical period of Africa. These parts delineate how the African has been alienated from the land first, the wise imperialists who helped themselves to the land paying into the pockets a few whatever worth they conceived to it. Finally a class of African landlords was able to purchase the land. In the novelist's mind, the question of re-achieving the land for the Kenyan people through struggle remains. Thus in this novel, Ngugi's analysis is at the stage where class antagonism between the capitalist and the proletariat is polarised. He also feels that bright future for Kenya will come only at the end of a long and arduous class struggle.

Later Ngugi turned to theatre with his publication of *Ngaahika Ndeende* in1977 in Gikuyu. This later appeared in English as *I Will Marry When I Want*. The production of this play brought about his arrest. He thought that through Gikuyu, he would convey his message to larger audiences. This play concerns with his unflinching plea for revolution in Kenya. Gigunda who works on Kioi's Farm says:

> It was then,
> That the state of Emergency was declared over Kenya,
> Our patriots
> Men and women of
> Limuru and the whole country
> Were arrested!
> The emergency laws became very oppressive
> Our homes were burnt down
> We were jailed.
> We were taken to detention camps.
> Some of us were crippled through beatings
> Others were castrated
> Our women were raped with booties
> Our wives and daughters were raped before our eyes.[29]

The above lines show how the Europeans ruthlessly exploited the Africans during the colonial times. Towards the end of the play, all sing out thus:

> The trumpet of the message has been blown
> Let us preach to all our friends
> The trumpet of the message has been blown
> We changed to new songs

For the revolution is near. (115)

The above lines express Ngugi's uncompromising plea for revolution.

In 1980, his novel *Caitaani Hultharaba Ini* appeared in Gikuyu. The English translation of this novel as *Devil on the Cross* came out from Heinemann in 1982. He wrote it while detained by the government that tried to silence him. He took nearly one year to complete this novel. "*Devil on the Cross* discusses and records the Kenyan people's struggles against the neo-colonial form and stage of imperialism."[30]

This novel crystallises his viewpoint expressed in the first three novels. There is an ingenious blending of formalised realism and ironic satire. The scene in the cave mirrors the blazon confidence expressed by Comprador capitalist society in certain parts of Africa. So sure of themselves are the moneyed elite that they feel little need to think about their real methods and motives while the competition to crown Kenyan leading extortion is satirically described. The assertive, cocksure tone that emanates from the body of the meeting will be menacingly familiar to many readers. The novel opens with certain people in Illmorog who told the protagonist that it was "too disgraceful, too shameful that it should be concealed in the death's ever lasting darkness." (7)

The novel suddenly shifts to the journey in a mini bus taxi from Nairobi to Illmorog. During the period of journey, the driver and the five passengers discuss the social issues that form the central theme relating to them, to their own experiences in life and differing in their reactions and moral assumptions. These long realistic passages are punctuated by flashes of absurdity, as the various invitation cards to 'the Devil's Feast' in Illmorog are scrutinized. This bewildered the characters themselves but "from the start Ngugi succeeds in containing these extravagance within a single credible fictional world."[31]

A Barrel of Pen Ngugi's next work is a collection of essays on his resistance to repression in neo-colonial Kenya. This is dedicated to Oginga Odinga, George Wamware and other students who struggled for a new Kenya. In the 'preface' to the book, Victoria Britain comments on the main thrust of the book thus:

> Kenya today has moved a long way down the well-trodden path of American Clint states—intellectuals are in prison and exile, institution of learning, books and place are under light government control.[32]

The despicable state in Kenya is such that intellectuals and enlightened persons resist the repressed regime. Ngugi clamors for an anti imperialistic struggle of the Kenyan people. He expresses his anguish at the deteriorating situation in Kenya.

> Today questioning the presence of foreign military bases and personnel (British, Israel and U.S) on Kenyan soil is disloyalty questioning colonialism is seduction. Teaching the history of the Kenyan people's resistance to colonialism is seduction. Theoretical exposure of colonial culture is seduction. Questioning the exploited and the oppression of the peasants and workers is Marxism and hence treason. Questioning corruption in high places is a seduction.[33]

Ngugi's next book entitled *Decolonizing the Mind* appeared in 1986. This is dedicated to the writers who write in African languages and who maintain the dignity of the literature, culture, philosophy and other treasures carried by African languages. Like a surgeon, Ngugi makes a rigorous analysis of the situation in Kenya. The essays in the book—the language of African literature, the language of African theatre, the language of African fiction, the quest for relevance—form a single unit and preserve the dignity of the Africans and their literature. In Ngugi's own words, they summarize some of the issues in which he has been passionately involved for the last twenty years of his practice in fiction, theatre, and criticism and in teaching literature. In a nutshell, "it is a part of continuing debate all over the continent about the destiny of Africa."[34]

Other essays in the book deal with the theme of resistance to the repression of Kenyan government. It is primarily on the need for the Kenyan women, peasants, artists and others to struggle for the liberation of Kenya from colonialism and neo-colonialism. Here, one is reminded of Peter Nazareth's *The General is up* where the author takes a quotation form Ishmael Reed's *The Last Louisiana Red*. Louisiana Red saw the way they were related to one another,

> oppressed one another, maimed and murdered one another, carving one another while above their head fifty thousand feet, billionaires flew in custom-made jet planes equipped with saunas tennis-courts, swimming-pools, discotheques and meeting rooms decorated a Marv. Griggin Snow set.[35]

Ngugi looks at the African realities as they are affected by the great struggle between the two mutually opposed forces in Africa, viz. an imperialistic tradition on the one hand and a 'resistance tradition' on the other. The former is maintained by the African neo-colonial bourgeois that controls the resistive population through police boots, barbed wire, a gowned clergy and judiciary. The resistance tradition is carried out by the working people (the peasantry and the proletariat) aided by patriotic students, intellectuals (academic and non-academic) soldiers and other progressive elements of the petty middle class.

Ngugi's interest in conveying his deep-felt convictions continued and he wrote a novel entitled *Matigari* in Gikuyu which was later translated by Wanguy wa Goro. As in the past even in this novel, Ngugi becomes critical of neo-colonialists that indulged in the exploitation of the Kenyans. He also expresses his genuine interest in African language, culture and tradition. Rightly does he dedicate this novel "to all those committed to the development of literature in the language of all the African people."[36]

The protagonist in *Matigari* doesn't approve of the people who sell out to the traitors. He is very much interested in serving the Kenyans. He becomes critical of the people who blindly follow the rulers. He says:

> There are two worlds. There is the world of those who accept things as they are and there is that of those who want to change things. (91)

Throughout the novel *Matigari* it is revealed that Ngugi's interest in "peasants, freedom fighters, revolutionary and above all the forces committed to building a new tomorrow." (126)

He earnestly feels that justice for the oppressed springs from the armed might of the people. The authorities in the end chase him but cannot capture him. The novel ends with Matigari's felt presence by every one in the country.

Ngugi is a committed writer with his own definite views on the art of fiction. His interest in what he sees around and his reaction to it has brought him to the sphere of drama and fiction. Naturally, he is an intensely committed writer with definite views on fiction and theatre. This is made clear from the interviews he has given of various journals and critics. According to him, "the role of an African novelist is to delve deep into the collective unconscious of his people to seek to the root, the trend in the revolutionary struggle."[37]

He says that a creative artist is obliged to peasants and workers. According to him, the post-Independence Kenya has not brought about any radical change in the country. He is of the opinion that in the post-Independence Kenya, the new African readers have become worse than the Europeans. So he laments on the lack of change in Kenya. He cries out thus:

> What have these peasants gained from 'Uhuru' has our ruling elite tried to change the colonial economic structure of the peasants and workers in control of the land they have fought for. . . . When I look around me, I see sad faces. I see unfulfilled hope and promise.[38]

As a creative artist, Ngugi vehemently advocates fights for a serious study of indigenous African languages and literature along side other literatures in English. He expresses his fervent hope in the African tradition thus:

> The African tradition, a tradition as active and alive as ever, constitutes the most significant influence. This is the stuff on which it grew up and it is the base from which we make our cultural take off into the world.[39]

These lines reveal to us his interest in 'black dimensions' that give validity to his writing. He did not hesitate to accept Caribbean literature where references have been made to the blacks who have suffered doubly under colonialism, capitalism, first as part of all the working masses and then as blacks. This black dimension and his socialist ideas put him in a position to be sympathetic to the needs of East Africa. He is of the opinion that a whole radical outlook in literature can be found by studying "representative works which mirror their society rather than to study a few isolated classics either of their own or of foreign culture."[40]

As a preserver of the African tradition, he wrote his later works in Gikuyu. He is of the opinion that language is a carrier of peoples' culture, culture is the carrier of peoples' values. By destroying people's language, you are destroying a very important aspect of their language. According to him, imperialism did this. Imperialism wanted to control the economy of African people:

> To do this they instituted political control but in history, economic control and political control have never been complete without culture or mental control. Because once you control how people look at themselves, you can in fact make a move in any other direction; you know, you can plant in them a slave mentality.[41]

Imperialism tried this through the suppression of people's songs, the suppression of the whole area of what is now called oral literature or Orature. So he sees writing by African people as part of the whole process of reclaiming the economic and political basis of their identity and he feels that language is very important in the process. There may be many different languages but we should be proud of that heritage and the beauty of our languages. *Moving the Centre: The Struggle for Cultural Freedom*, published in 1993, reflects these ideas. He wrote in Gikuyu to reach his people. In his own words,

> When I write in Gikuyu at least some peasants and workers will read my work when I write in English not even a single one of them will read the work. . . . It is more important to encourage

> people to be proud of their mother tongue, then you can be proud of also languages which are closer to you and so forth.[42]

Ngugi's characters are drawn primarily from Kenyan society. He talks about the characters whom he knows and who have expressed their agony. He says:

> I was talking with my own people. I was talking with the characters that I knew in a way who had agonies, which I have seen with our own people in Kenya.[43]

As a novelist, Ngugi, like Conrad, creates the characters who would question and attack the establishment. He also appreciated any character that grows by becoming inquisitive. Mostly his characters are drawn from the Kenyan society. He says, "I wrote in Gikuyu because, I was talking with my own people."[44]

His recent novel, *Wizard of the Crow*, is written in Gikuyu and is yet to be translated into English. It is written in nearly thousand pages and was published in 2004. After twenty-two years of exile, he came to Kenya but he was brutally attacked and robbed by some gang in Nairobi. His wife was raped. He suspects the political hand behind it. But, he is determined to continue his writings. By identifying himself with the Kenyan society and its history he delineates various facets of exploitation in his country. He draws our attention to the growing awareness among the Kenyans of the importance of education. He says:

> The Gikuyus have always seen education as a means to greater prosperity and when the white man came to Kenya and took away the land and ruled the people, they said to themselves the white man can do this because he has got education, now if we also can get education then we can get the things which he had.[45]

As a writer with commitment, he feels that the history of Kenya has been one of racial tensions and racial quarrels. This is discussed in the first three published novels. As a writer one should not "stand a little bit detached but he should see the problem, the human problem, and the human relationship in its proper perspective."[46]

These lines reveal to us his commitment to Kenyan society. As a creative writer, he feels that he should discuss the problems of the Kenyan society, record varied kinds of exploitation meted out to them, their revolutionary urge to transform society by violence in colonial and neo-colonial Kenya. A study will be made of the element of exploitation that is evident in the six published novels of Ngugi.

NOTES

1. Kofi Awoonor, "James Ngugi, Ferdinand Oyono and Anti-Colonial Novel," *The Breast of the Earth; A Survey of History, Culture and Literature of Africa* (Enuju: Nok. Publishers, 1975), p. 282.
2. Allan Marcuson, Mike Gonzalez and Dave Williams, "James Ngugi Interviewed by Fellow Students at Leeds University," *CUL*, 31 (1961), p. 2.
3. *Ibid.*, p. 123.
4. Cosmos Pieterse and Denis Duerden, *African Writers Talking* (London: Heinemann Educational Books, 1972), p. 122.
5. *Ibid.*, p. 123.
6. G.D. Killam, *An Introduction to the Writings of Ngugi wa Thiong'o* (London: Heinemann, 1980), p. 17.
7. Swen Poulsen, "African History from a European Point of View," *Kunapipi*, Vol. 3, No. 1, 1981, p. 84.
8. Read Personal Interview with Michael Okenimkpe, *The Weekly Review* (Nairobi, 17 Feb. 1975), p. 12.
9. Ngugi wa Thiong'o, *Homecoming* (London: Heinemann, 1972), p. 149-50.
10. Jomo Kenyatta, *Facing Mount Kenya* (London: Martin Secker and Warburg, 1938), p. 317.
11. Pieterse and Duerden, p. 128.
12. *Ibid.*, p. 129.
13. *Ibid.*, p. 122.
14. Kirsten Holst Peterson, "Birth Pangs of a National Consciousness, Mau Mau and Ngugi wa Thiong'o," *WLWE*, Vol. 26, No. 2 (1981), p. 214.
15. Yohana, "More than Politics," *Kenya Weekly News*, August 4, 1961), p. 30.
16. Bernth Lindfors, "Ngugi wa Thiongo's Early Journalism," *WLWE*, Vol. 20, No. 1 (Spring 1981), p. 32.

17. Ngugi wa Thiong'o, *The Black Hermit* (London: Heinemann, 1968), p. VIII.
18. Bailey Millard, "Rabindranath Tagore Discovers America," *The Bookman*, Vol. 44, No. 1916, pp. 244-51.
19. Killam, p. 14.
20. Walt Whitman, "On the Beach at Night," *American Literature of Nineteenth Century*, ed. William J. Fisher et al. (New Delhi: Urasia, 1964), p. 381.
21. David Cook and Michael Okenimkpe, *Ngugi wa Thiong'o: An Exploration of His Writings* (London: Heinemann, 1983), p. 27.
22. Corinthians, *The Holy Bible*, Book 1, Chapter 15, Line 36.
23. *Ibid.*, p. 36.
24. Austin. S. Bukenya, "A Review of the Literature of East and Central Africa," *Journal of Commonwealth Literature*, No. 80, 1969, pp. 12-17.
25. Killam, p. 84.
26. Ngugi wa Thiong'o and Micere Githae Mugo, *The Trial of Dedan Kimathi* (London: Heinemann, 1976), p. viii.
27. Derek Walcott, *The Castaway and Other Poems* (London: Jonathan Cape, 1963).
28. Ngugi wa Thiong'o, Interview by Magina Magina, *African Report*, No. 9, February 1979, pp. 30-31.
29. Ngugi wa Thiong'o, *I Will Marry When I Want* (London: Heinemann, 1982) p. 27.
30. Ngugi wa Thiong'o, *Detained: A Prisoner's Dairy* (London: Heinemann, 1981), p. 8.
31. Cook and Okenimkpe, p. 124.
32. Ngugi wa Thiong'o, *A Barrel of Pen: Resistance to Repression in Neocolonial Kenya* (New York: African World Press, 1983), p. 2.
33. *Ibid.*, p. ix.
34. Ngugi wa Thiong'o, *Decolonising the Mind: The Politics of Language in African Literature* (London: James Curey, 1986), p. 1.
35. Peter Nazereth, *The General Is Up* (Calcutta: Writers Workshop, 1984), p. 1.
36. Ngugi wa Thiong'o, "Preface," *Matigari* (London: HEB, 1987), p. 6.
37. Ngugi, *Homecoming*, p. 46.
38. *Ibid.*, p. 49.
39. *Ibid.*, p. 89.
40. *Ibid.*, p. 149.

41. Ngugi wa Thiong'o, Interviewed by Hansel Nolumbeyoh, *Journal of Commonwealth Literature*, p. 164.
42. Ngugi wa Thiong'o, Interviewed by Denis Deurden, *African Writers Talking*, ed. Denis Deurden and Cosmo Pietesse, p. 123.
43. *Ibid.*, p. 123.
44. Ngugi wa Thiong'o, interviewed by Ameenu Abdullahi, *African Writers Talking*, ed. Denis Deurden and Cosmo Pietesse, p. 126.
45. *Ibid.*
46. *Ibid.*, p. 128.

Chapter 3

Exploitation of the Africans by the Europeans

Ngugi is a writer who is intensely dedicated to the advocacy of certain beliefs and programs especially, pertaining to his own African community. His beliefs emanate from his sense of moral fervour, conviction and righteousness. He, in his works, records the exploitation of the Africans at the hands of the Europeans:

> I believe that African intellectuals alien themselves with the struggle of the African message for a meaningful national ideal. . . . The African writer can help in articulating the feelings behind the struggle.[1]

These lines reveal Ngugi's sensitiveness to the society around him and his concern for shaping and moulding his community.

Ngugi in his fictional works delineates vividly the exploitation of the Africans by the Whites and the consequential crippling effect of such exploitation on the lives of the Africans. He broadly identifies three facets of encounter of the Africans with the European imperialists—slavery, colonialism and neocolonialism. His first three novels—*Weep Not, Child* and *The River Between* and *A Grain of Wheat*—deal with the period of slavery and colonialism. In *Petals of Blood*, *Devil on the Cross* and *Matigari*, though the emphasis is on neo-colonialism, the other two facets are also identified no less conspicuously. G.D. Killam says, "obviously here is a good deal of overlapping in the novels in the way in which the three phases, Ngugi identifies are treated."[2]

Before depicting in his fictional world various methods by which the Whites exploited the Africans, Ngugi describes at length in his first novel, *The River Between*, the impenetrable Kenya in all its beauty. Then he explains how the Kenyans had been without any fear of intrusion by '*Ukabi*' (outsider) leading a happy, peaceful and united life with their traditions and customs which bound them to their land. The African people believed that the land on which they lived was their God, Murunga's gift to their first parents—Gikuya and Mumbi. Murunga showed them the vast fertile land and told them: "This land, I give it to you, oh, man and woman. It is yours to rule and till, you and your posterity." (*RB*, 2)

The River Between begins with Ngugi's assertion that the fertile land of Kenya belonged basically to the Africans. Mugo wa Kabiro, one of the great seers of old who had been all over the Gikuyu country prophesied the invasion of the Gikuyu country by the Whiteman thus: "There shall come a people with clothes like butterflies." (2)

Chege, who was a 'respected man' of the ridges, a believed descendent of Mugo wa Kabiro, also predicted the arrival of the White man and told the people of the ridges that the Whites had already set up their houses and have taken their land in the neighbouring places of Murungu, Nyeri and Kiambo. But people refused to give credence to their words. Though the railway line laid by the Whites ran across the country, the people not knowing this whispered: "The White man cannot speak the languages of hills. And knows not the ways of the land" (7). The Africans, due to their ignorance, and deep belief in their impenetrable nature of the hills could not forestall the incoming invaders from settling down with their religious missionary at Siriana, a place situated at the outskirts of Makuyu and Kameno ridges. Ngugi "succeeds in evoking the atmosphere of the ridges and chronicling the traditions and customs they embrace."[3]

These Whites soon occupied the surrounding land and with their religious preaching and catechism, they were able to convert to their faith quite a few natives like Joshua and Kabonyi. The act of conversion is the first step of colonialism.

Livingstone, the leading missionary, visited the hills only occasionally to give new life and energy to his followers. He made Joshua, the black convert whom he used as his agent to carry on his main work of preaching to the Africans about the existence of one God—Jesus. Through Joshua, a firm and capable preacher, Livingstone was able to convert many Africans to take to the new faith shedding their faith in the native religion. Because of the new faith, the old conformity of the African society was broken. This is brought out symbolically by Ngugi through Joshua's building:

> The round thatched huts standing in groups of three or four convey a picture of conformity broken only by Joshua's house which has a tin roof and is rectangular. The very presence of the house is an indication that the old isolation of Makuyu from the rest of the world was being broken down. (28)

The preaching of new ways and values of life through a new religion had a drastically adverse effect on the old beliefs. The collision between the two antagonistic ways of life was indeed most catastrophic and tragic. Ngugi remarkably portrays in *The River Between* the tragic predicament of the Kenyans torn by a lacerating conflict between the loss of cultural heritage and identity in the exploitative colonial context at both the individual and societal levels. Thus "the disinheritance of the Gikuyu religion and tribal culture by White colonialism figures in this novel."[4]

The Whites began to pour into the interior in large numbers. The newly built railway line, the settled land of the Whites around Siriana mission and ever-increasing number of converts eased their way to spread further.

The impenetrable thick line that distinguished the outsider from the insider became penetrable. The White people as well as the Indians started business on Kenyan land. The White government began to run from Siriana. The government administrators were not seen directly but were heard through the missionaries. This was announced to the Makuyu ridges that a government post was soon going to be established there and that the people would be ruled from there. Missionary people also spoke of the taxes the natives had to pay to the White government in Nairobi.

The lands being intact then, the native people did not take serious notice of the ways of the Whites or of the taxes being imposed by them.

Siriana missionary centre also started a school. Chege, who believed in the ancient prophecy of Mugo that salvation would come from the blood that flowed in him, thought of imparting his knowledge to his son Waiyaki, whom he named after the great Gikuyu warrior. He told him:

> Arise, Head the prophecy. Go to Mission place, learn all the wisdom and all the secretes of the White man. But do not follow his vices. Be true to your people and ancient rituals. (20)

Chege's speech resembled Ezelu's speech to his son in Chinua Achebe's *The Arrow of God*. Both followed the universal principle according to which the subject class learned those tricks of the aggressor and used them against the aggressor himself. It was not only the belief of Chege but also of many traditional Africans at the time of religious conflicts. They believed that White man's magic lay in education. They were not able to realise the kind of education that was imparted at Siriana missionary centre. As Robson says: "The learning and wisdom that the pupils hope to acquire has much potential to destroy the old ways as to preserve them by fighting the White man with his own weapons." (7)

The novelist does not hesitate to draw attention to the theme of exploitation in the field of education imparted by the colonisers. The education imparted to the students in the Siriana missionary school was directed mainly to advance the interests of the British Empire. They wanted to convert the Africans to believe in their faith and assist them to spread their religion. They also wanted the students to help them in the administration of the natives. Thus, Livingstone pinned his hopes on Waiyaki and saw in him 'a possible Christian leader of the Church.' Education directed to these purposes asserted the supremacy of their religion and began to condemn the native rituals, customs and traditions. Ngugi comments thus:

> A is sitting on B . . . what kind of education will A want B to set? In other words, education what kind of culture and consciousness? 'A' will want 'B' to believe that he, B has no culture or his culture is inferior. 'A' will want 'B' to imbibe a culture inculcates in his values of self-doubt and self-denigration, in a word a slave consciousness. He will now look up to A, a superior culture.[5]

Livingstone and his missionary people considered the traditional customs as satanic works. They called the Gikuyu God, 'the prince of darkness.' At Siriana it was taught thus:

> Those who refuse him are the children of darkness;
> These, sons and daughters of evil one, will go to Hell;
> They will burn and burn forever more, world unending. (*RB*, 29)

These 'strong words' frightened converts like Joshua. It is said that Joshua's whole body shook 'to the very roots of his being.' It is only when he was baptized that he felt at peace and stopped 'trembling.' The effect of such preaching was so much on Joshua that he repented all his life for having married circumcised Miriamu. He did not like his children to undergo such rituals. He felt that they would get contaminated even if they listened to the initiation songs. Having got thoroughly influenced by foreign religion, he began preaching to the people to believe in the *Bible* and give up the traditions. By condemning the native tradition in favour of the new faith and by becoming a preacher himself, he was at once the exploited as well as the exploiter.

Chege witnessed the strength of the strange forces of new faith, which influenced many Africans to get converted. He was disappointed that he was not able to do anything in his lifetime. He feared if his son, Waiyaki, too might begin to dislike the ways of the ridge and its rituals. In fact, he had pinned great hopes on his son that he would be the saviour of the ridge. Though Waiyaki did not condemn the rituals, as Joshua did, the impact of missionary education was clearly seen on him on the day before circumcision. At first, he stood, as an outsider, though he liked to be involved like other boys of his age. He grew uneasy to listen to the songs of circumcision sung by the young Kenyan boys and girls of his age. Later, when he was pushed into the circle dancing around the fire, his body mechanically moved rhythmically according to the music of the whistles and horns but the voice of White man's education made him guilty and he could not put his soul in it. In fact, he remembered Livingstone and what he might have felt about it. Ngugi comments on the disruptive influence of Christianity on the African life thus:

> Christianity as an organized religion is corrupt and hypocritical: besides acting as an agent of imperialism, It exercised a highly disruptive influence on African life and was the chief villain in alienating the African from his own culture.[6]

Waiyaki who could not make a choice between two conflicting faiths in the community suffered between two loyalties. Despite being the son of Chege who was well versed in the significance of every ritual of the tribes, Waiyaki became subjugated under the influence of the missionary people and the White man's education. Muthoni, the younger daughter of Joshua was not completely carried away by her father's principles that condemned the rituals of the tribe. Like Waiyaki, she too believed that the ritual of the circumcision was important to the people who lived there. But unlike him, she was able to participate fully in the celebrations of circumcision. At the same time, she believed in the foreign faith her parents had embraced. Waiyaki was surprised to know that Muthoni revolted against her father's will to get circumcised. He could not think of being a rebel placing himself in Muthoni's place. With his subjugated mind, he was unable to make a clear choice and hence the chances of his becoming a successful saviour become less. In fact, he always felt 'a stranger to his land' and behaved detachedly from the politics of the land.

Ngugi makes circumcision the central point around which he rotates his novel and describes in a telling manner the cultural exploitation of the Africans by Whites. Robson comments: "In his narration of the ceremony of circumcision, he draws a number of elements closely together." (8) In chapters III and IV of *The River Between*, Ngugi describes at length the importance of the circumcision to the people who lived there. He makes it explicitly clear that the act of circumcision is the most central in the Gikuyu way of life.

> Circumcision was an important ritual to the tribe. It kept the people together, bound the tribe. It was the core of the social structure and something that gave meaning to a man's life. End the custom and spiritual bias of the tribe's cohesion and integration would be no more. (79)

Obsessed with the foreign faith, Joshua forgot fatherly love towards his daughter Muthoni, when she got infected after cleriodectomy, and disowned her for following traditional faith of the land. Even when her health deteriorated, he did not move: on the other hand, he wanted to plant a curse on her and finally when she died, he thought that she deserved it for following satanic ritual. This he thought would teach a lesson to the traditional people who followed it. The early convert "had to prove how Christian he was through rejection of his past roots . . . so that in Kenya . . . the missionary robbed people of their soul."[7] The death of Muthoni had far-reaching consequences. Livingstone, earlier, believed in gradual eradication of the traditional customs of the Africans. In spite of pressure by his higher authorities at home and in Kenya, he refused to adopt rash and desperate measures. But he realised, after his twenty-five years of stay in Kenya, that he was not making much progress. Now, Muthoni's death 'for ever confirmed the barbarity of Gikuyu customs.' He thought:

> Circumcision had to be rooted out if there was to be any hope of salvation for these people . . . it was Christ who would be fighting the Princes of Darkness through him. (56)

He began to adopt vigorous methods to suppress the Gikuyu customs and decreed a law that circumcised Africans are not allowed to missionary school. He called his African agents, Joshua and Kabonyi to help him. Now, 'the war was on.' *The River Between* is "the Blackman's sense of insecurity, his sense of threat to his environs and to his mode and method of life."[8]

Joshua became more jealous and adamant in preaching Christian doctrines. Unable to follow completely the new faith, many converts alienated from Livingstone and Joshua, the pro-Christian leader. A new political organization, 'Kiama' was raised to safeguard the traditions. Just as Joshua condemned everything traditional, Kiama condemned everything that belonged to the White man. The people of Kameno and those of Mykuyu ridges, who followed two different faiths, moved away from each other. Thus conflicts and splits occurred not only in the psyche of the individuals but also in the society. One is reminded of Chinua Achebe's *Things Fall Apart* which sums up the African religion thus:

> How can he when he does not even speak our tongue? but he says that our customs are bad; and our own brothers. He came quietly and peacefully with his religion. We were amused at his foolishness and allowed him to stay. Now he has won our brothers, and our clan can no longer be like one. He has put a knife on the things that held us together and we have fallen apart.[9]

The people of the ridges ceased to talk to each other. 'The clear edges of life' as Waiyaki called them had completely disappeared under the impact of White man's religious attitude towards the natives.

According to the missionary laws decreed, circumcised Africans are not allowed to their schools and so Waiyaki, as a circumcised person, could not carry on his studies. Therefore, he started a new school—the first one of its kind in the area. He was obsessed with the power of Whites' education just as Joshua was obsessed with the foreign religious faith. Both were the exploited products of White man's twin tools—religion and education. Waiyaki shunned all forms of politics and refused even to support the 'Kiama' activity in spite of taking the oath earlier, for they might come on his way to educate the people. As the author says:

> Perhaps the preaching of Livingstone, that education was of value and his boys should not concern themselves with what the gov-

> ernment was doing of politics, had found a place in Waiyaki's heart. (65)

Having been a product of such exploitative educational system, he could not see nor understand the politics of the time. In the process to educate the people of the ridges, he had not even been able to see the increasing influence of 'Kiama' to fit into his scheme of things. Neither was he able to see the danger that was going to fall on him. In fact, White man's education acted as a hidden wound for him.

Waiyaki tried to reconcile the Christian faith with the traditional faith of the land. The essence of education was to him a clarion call to unite all the people and to drive out the White settlers. He remembered the nature of work his father had assigned to him in the journey after circumcision. But preoccupied with his education, he lost the track of his goal to ensure 'unity' between the ridges and to preach 'reconciliation.' Waiyaki appeared to be in a state of confusion—the confusion created by the Europeans with their religion and education.

The novelist creates the tragic story of love between the uncircumcised beautiful elder daughter of pro-Christian Joshua and the circumcised educated son of traditional Chege. After the death of his younger daughter, Joshua was preoccupied with preaching Christian principles vigorously to the people and did not notice the change in his elder daughter who grew vexed with his new faith that has no humanity. She thought:

> If the faith of Joshua and Livingstone came to separate; why, it was not good. If it came to stand between a father and his daughter so that her death did not move him, then it was inhuman. She wanted the other. (134)

That other was her love for Waiyaki. Thus White man's religion has blinded the early convert Joshua. His family was completely disintegrated when Nyambura walked out with Waiyaki proclaiming openly her love for him in the presence of the people who came to listen to Joshua's Christian preach. It was a lapse on the part of Joshua, who as a parent and preacher was not able to bring up his children in the light of his new faith. He always wanted to show to the people that his was an ideal family and he would set an example to others. But what actually happened made him eat an humble pie.

According to the tradition, uncircumcised man or woman was not eligible to marry within the tribe. Leaders of Kiama wanted the people to punish Waiyaki for violating the oath of Kiama so that other people did not commit similar sacrilege. Waiyaki saw in the union of the two sides a reconciliation of the two faiths. But the people were not ready to judge it that way. They were confused about the religious conflicts that arose because of the new faith. Ngugi presents graphically the confused state when the two lovers were placed for the judgement before Kiama.

> The crowd roared back 'yes' as if the burden of judging their teacher were removed from them they went away quickly glad that he was hidden by the darkness. For they did not want to look at the teacher and they did not want to read the guilt of one another faces. (152)

The dilemma of the masses to make a choice between traditionalism and the new faith leads to utter confusion and as a result tragedies occurred. Werner Glinga says that the novelist sees "this confusion as the key to understand Kenyan history from the beginning of European intrusion and sets out to explore with the benefit of hindsight, how the people of the early colonial period came to misunderstand the options of their time and to confuse their vital interest. Ngugi's idea of African hero of colonial occupation originates in the pre-independence pro-literary tradition in Kenya."[10] These lines show the impact of cultural exploitation of the Whites on the Africans. Thus in *The River Between*, Ngugi presents the picture of a Gikuyu hero who stands as a weak-willed person after the havoc played by the European colonies in Kenya.

II

The theme of exploitation of the colonised through missionary education recurs in *Weep Not, Child* another powerful novel of Ngugi. T.N. Dhar comments: "In *Weep Not, Child* the weeping child is at the centre of the novel for he has the fear of being exploited at the hands of others. Naturally, the child Njoroge has the sympathy of the author for him."[11]

In *Weep Not, Child*, Njoroge is advised by his father Ngotho to join missionary school of Siriana. Promoted by all the members of his house, Njoroge saw himself destined for something big: "Njoroge did not want to be like his father working for a white man, or, worst for an Indian." (49) He had heard and seen the hardship of his father. He would escape through his education from such conditions and have his brothers and mothers to escape from such poor conditions and hardship that they were facing now.

Njoroge's desire to get himself educated became more intense and he actually saw himself as a possible saviour of the whole God's country through his education. Soon he became a slave to the western values that cut him off from his native roots. He was also tuned by the influence of the Bible, which was taught as part of education at the school. The Bible became his favourite book and it brought about a change in his vision of life thus:

> His belief in a future for his family and the village rested then not only on a hope for sound education but also on a belief in a God of love and mercy, who long ago walked on this earth with Gikuyu and Mumbi, or Adam and Eve. (55)

His sense of justice was tuned up by the principles of missionary education. He traced the oppressed Kenyans as those children of Israel about whom he read in the Bible. He began to believe in the brotherhood of the Whites and the blacks. This education made him not to look upon the Whites who occupied their lands as his enemies. With this subjugated mind, Njoroge was not able to fight for the lands occupied by the colonisers. He, like Waiyaki, had put too much of faith in education as a weapon against the exploiters but in the process, he himself became the exploiter.

In the hour of need, when his father was dead and all his three brothers were imprisoned, it was not Njoroge's education that rescued them, it was Kamau who helped them financially. All Njoroge's vision of childhood vanishes when he, forced by strained circumstances, sought to work in an Indian shop. He looked pathetically at the children going to school with their faces gleaming with hope.

> He too had once been like this when he had seen the world as a place where a man with learning would rise to power and glory. Then he would never have thought that he would even work for an Indian. . . . The children were frightened by his blank stare, they scampered away. (146)

Njoroge was removed from the shop as he did not prove to be a successful salesman. His hope 'Sun will rise tomorrow' became a mere illusion. He felt that western education made him a coward, an old man at the age of twenty. If only he had learnt any thing other than missionary education that would teach him to earn his livelihood like Kamau, his life would have taken a different turn and he too would have become useful to his family and society.

> He is like Blitzer, the boy (in *Hard Times*) only knows a horse in words as a mental abstraction. . . . His education has been used to mystify and obscure reality.[12]

Ngugi through young and sensitive Njoroge revealed the exploitative nature of the White colonial education and its drastic effect on the minds of the young Kenyan children who were to grow into responsible Kenyan citizens. He exemplified Wayaki's realisation at the end of the novel, *Weep Not Child*, that 'education for oppressed people is not all.'

III

Munira, in Ngugi's *Petals of Blood*, becomes a victim of the imposed foreign faith. Munira, the son of brother Ezekiel wa Weru, felt that the new faith has no relevance to the situation in which he was living. When he was young, he attended circumcision ritual without the knowledge of his father. There he met

Wanziru singing and dancing in one of the circumcision dances. He fell in love with her and married her. But after the marriage she changed over to a Christian name as Julia under the influence of Munira's father and became a good Christian daughter-in-law. Munira did not like her praying in a Christian fashion even when she was in the bed with him. So he had the feeling of 'emptiness' in him. He ran away to Illmorog in search of something to fill the emptiness. In the novel, Munira's feelings are rightly observed thus:

> But even with Wanja he found that he was still a prisoner of his own upbringing and Siriana missionary education. It was not that he did not enjoy the experience, on the contrary despite that upbringing he knew that there was nothing so great, nothing so joyous as those few seconds of expectation before entry into a woman unknown. (72)

These lines show how Munira became a victim to the colonial religion and education. Ngugi continues to record the oppressed feelings of the Africans. Siriana School produced corrupt officials like Chui, Nderiwa, Kimaria who exploited their fellow Africans. Munira blamed Cambridge Fraudsham, the headmaster of the Siriana School. Fraudsham wanted to mould his people to be sincere subjects of the British Empire to subserve its interest. He played tough with African students, made them salute the British flag everyday and pray in chorus:

> Wash me Redeemer and I shall be Whiter than snow we would then pray for the continuation of an empire that has defeated the satanic evil which has erupted in Europe to try the children of God. (29)

Thus Fraudsham in his capacity as the head of Siriana School worked towards the perpetuation of the White domination while the Kenyans associated education with advancement of political freedom and even economic freedom. The colonial education was meant to obscure realism, and other forms of oppression. The purpose and content of imperialist education was thoroughly scrutinised and its relevance to the African situation was questioned throughout the novel. These evil effects of colonial education are powerfully described in his *Petals of Blood*.

Most of the Christians depicted in Ngugi's fictional works were unsympathetic to their fellow human beings in Kenya and they behaved as the White man's lackeys. For example in *Petals of Blood* the Reverend Jerrod Brown, the pastor of the 'All Saints Church' in New Illmorog turned away the hungry, famished and ailing villagers from palatial home in a most unchristian fashion. He instead of providing the crowds with food, discusses at length spiritual illness thus:

> What the *Bible* is talking about is not so much a physical illness as a spiritual condition. For, note that the man never went inside the temple until he was cured of his spiritual lameness . . . the *Bible* is then clearly against life of idleness and begging. This is what is wrong with the country. (148)

Colonial education taught the Africans about western conquerors, inventors, discoverers, writers and Livingstones. It wanted Africans to look up Livingstones as their saviours while Mau Mau patriots were portrayed as terrorists. When Karega in *Petals of Blood* went through the history of Africa, he only found Africans described as wanderers who had no civilization. They were considered as primitives and uncivilized people. But they covered up their unequal treatment. Karega said that the writers of history were obedient to the imperialistic masters. He lamented that their past had a broken civilization because of the Whites' cultural exploitation. Gatuiria in *Devil on the Cross* reiterated the same idea as Karega did in *Petals of Blood*. As an African research student in culture, he was sorry that their ancestors' wisdom and philosophy had to take a back seat in the foreigners' dispensation. The natives were not even able to find books in their national languages. Their native songs, riddles, stories, customs, traditions and everything about African heritage had been lost to them. Gathuiria says, "they cannot go anywhere to know the history of their country. They are left like a child without parents to counsel them." (58)

IV

Africans not only suffered the loss of their culture but also lost their lands to the Europeans during the colonial times. Ngugi portrays the political and the economic exploitation of the Africans by the Europeans in his fictional works.

Ngugi describes in *Weep Not, Child*, how the colonists exploited the natives by depriving them of the ownership of their lands and reducing them to the miserable state of workers at their behest on those lands. Waiyaki in *The River Between* had felt:

> the shame of people land being taken away the shame of being forced to work on those same lands, the humiliation of paying taxes to a government that you know nothing about. (*RB*, 164)

These things which are mentioned casually in *The River Between* occupy the centrestage in *Weep Not, Child*. By the time the novel opens, there are already many natives working in settled areas and in foreign shops to make their living and there is a clear demarcation of the fertile lands occupied by the Whites from those allotted for the blacks. The novelist depicts the confrontation between Whites and Blacks and the alienation of the land. "You could tell the land of Black People because it was red, rough and stickly, while the land of the white settlers was green and was not lacerated into small strips." (8)

In Kenya, a person with land was considered to be rich than a person with a lot of other material wealth. It was because a majority of the people live as peasants. The Kenyans had a holistic attachment to the land which satiates them both materially and spiritually. Jomo Kenyatta describes the Gikuyu belief in this way:

> the Gikuyu consider the earth as the mother of tribe . . . it is the soil that feeds the child through a lifetime; and again after death it is the soil that nurses the spirit of the dead for eternity. Thus the earth is the most sacred thing above all that dwell in or on it. Among the Gikuyu the soil is especially honored and an everlasting oath is to swear by the earth.[13]

Naturally, therefore, any loss of land constituted the greatest misfortune and suffering to a Kenyan. Ngugi's main concern in his novels is the dispossession of the Kenyans of their land. Kamau in *Weep Not, Child* says:

> Yes. Black people have their land in the country of black people. White men have their land in their own country. It is simple. I think it was God's plan (49)

This is reiterated by Ngugi thus:

> I believe that every Kenyan has a right to decent food and decent clothing, I believe no Kenyan should be able to sleep with any peace of mind for as long as he knows that what he is feeding upon had been taken from the mouths of thirsty and hungry in Kenya. I also believe that no Kenyan should be able to sleep peacefully for as long as he knows that the wealth of the country is still controlled by foreign merchants.[14]

The Whites did not conquer the whole of Kenyan land. They dispossessed Kenyans of their lands during the two great wars. Ngotho narrated to the barber, how he had become a '*Muhoi*' on his own lands thus:

> It was the first big war. . . . All of us were taken by force. We made roads. . . . The war ended. . . . My father and many others had been moved from our ancestral lands. He died lonely, a poor man waiting for the white man to go. The white did not go and he died a *Muhoi* on this very land. (29)

Colonists continued their exploitation of the Africans even during the war. They promised that after coming back from the war, they would give back to the Africans the land they occupied. On the contrary, they occupied even more land by the time the Africans returned from the war. They did not fulfil their promise to the natives even after the Second World War. Howlands exploited Ngotho's attachment to his lands, made him work on low wages and made good profit. Ngugi puts forth his views on the double exploitation of the blacks by the Whites thus:

> Black people have been victims of double exploitation. They have been exploited on the level of the working class and the labouring

> masses. They have also been exploited on the dimension of race because of the whole colonial context in which black and White people have met.[15]

Boro, the son of Ngotho, poured out his anger against exploitative settlers and government thus:

> The land has been taken away, through the *Bible* and sword . . . the *Bible* paved the way for the sword . . . their forefathers pitied the stranger and welcomed him with open arms into their fold. (65)

Boro and his brothers were not left with land to live on it. Ngotho's sons were scattered to make their living. Ngotho is aware of the fact that Howlands is responsible for his poor economic conditions. "How long do you think I can endure this drudgery, for the sake of a white man and his children?" (60)

Howlands's exploitative and suppressive attitude is brought out clearly during the emergency. When Ngotho joined the strike to get back his occupied lands back, Howlands wanted "to bring Ngotho to a submissive humiliation. . . . This would be the crowning glory to his career." (111)

Howlands's economic condition was not good before Ngotho joined as a worker in his fields. It was only with his labour that Howlands grew rich. Instead of giving him reasonable wages, Howlands became aggressive and thought of putting him 'in the right position.' "For Ngotho, his White employer is the ever present perpetrator of the laws he has suffered."[16]

Howlands raised his African agent, Jacobo, to a chief's position to arrest Ngotho and his sons even on false allegations. Before Ngotho's very eyes, he got arrested Ngotho's wife and children. To Howlands, Ngotho became a symbol of evil that stood on his way in his possession of Ngotho's land.

Howlands as was the usual practice with government agents, took the law into his hands and harassed and ill-treated Ngotho to forcibly extract information from him about Jacobo's death. He treated Ngotho so cruelly that even the homeguards who worked with him got scared to be in the place where Howlands was harassing Ngotho. Finally, Howlands drove Ngotho to death after making him suffer both physically and mentally.

Howlands's selfish, exploitative nature was clearly exposed when he just utilised the services of Jacobo and did not care to protect him when his life was in danger. Indeed he set Africans against their fellow Africans. He thought:

> But he would use him. The very ability to set these people fighting amongst themselves instead of fighting with the white men gave him an amused satisfaction. (88)

He got Ngotho's family members arrested by Jacobo. Howlands's wife also indulges in exploitation of the African workers. Whenever Howlands was busy and neglected her, she abused the African farm workers and removed them from the work. She and her husband never were conscious that they were usurpers of Ngotho's land.

The White people arrested Jomo Kenyatta, the leader of the strike, and the people were deprived of the leadership for organising the strike. The government declared an Emergency. Fear gripped the Gikuyu land in the form of curfews, arrests, repressive measures and deaths. Njeri described how the Whites exploited the Africans through their draconian laws:

> The white man makes a law or a rule. Through that rule or law or what you may call it, he takes away the land and then imposes many laws on the people concerning that land and many other things, all without people agreeing first as in the old days of tribe. Now a man rises . . . who can win even if the angets of God were his lawyers. (84-85)

Ngugi portrayed how Muhoi's families were destroyed during the early emergency period by the White oppressive government and its exploitative laws.

In *A Grain of Wheat*, the intensity of exploitation by the Europeans during emergency period at its peak is graphically described. Howlands and Livingstone were the only prominent people in *Weep Not, Child* and *The River Between* respectively, but in *A Grain of Wheat*, the Europeans's number increased and with them the intensity of the exploitation of the natives also increased. Mr. Rogers, an agriculture officer, wanted to set up a forest research station in dark Africa but a train at Githima crushed him.

> A Forestry Research Station was set up in the area, not as a tribute to his martyrdom, but as part of a new colonial development plan. Soon Githima Forestry and Agricultural Research Station teemed with European scientists and administrators. (33)

Ngugi in *A Grain of Wheat* draws the attention of the readers to Thompson, a White representative in Kenya. Ime Ikeidden calls him, 'a firm grip of the European colonial type.' G.D. Killam says that in *A Grain of Wheat*: "There is a larger community of Whites British for the most part . . . and we see the forces of the belief in the civilizing mission with its emphasis as a benevolent paternalism. This theme is consolidated in John Thompson." (56) In this novel, Thompson easily becomes the exponent of the ethics of imperial colonialism: "Thompson embodies for Ngugi that most odious form of political authority, colonialism, so of all his characters it is on Thompson that he pours most scorn."[17]

For Thompson, colonisation is a process of civilizing the savages of the African continent. Indeed, he considered it as White man's burden. He was of the opinion that the darkness and the mystery of the forest led the primitive men to magic and rituals and condemned them all like Livingstone in *Weep Not, Child*. He firmly believed that it was with the effort of Europeans, the wild bushes were turned into modern cities. The irrationality, inconsistency and superstition of the Africans yielded place to the western principles of reason, order and measure. He planned to reorientate the African people towards the British way of living by altering their social and cultural environment. He held a high opinion about the British and their way of living.

> I was convinced that the growth of the British Empire was the development of a great moral idea . . . to be English was basically an attitude of mind: it was a way to looking at life, at human relationship, at the just ordering of human society. (54)

He enters into his diary a few lines from Dr. Albert Schweitzer: "The Negro is a child, and with children, nothing can be done without the use of authority." (55)

This idea coloured his attitudes and activities towards his fellow Africans. As colonial administrator, he became 'a symbol of unmovable White power' in Kenya. He considered the Mau Mau movement, which retorted his activities as the evil one that stood between him and his morals. Thompson considered himself as 'Prospero in Africa' and made attempts to suppress it cruelly. Those who did not co-operate with the White government were considered as Mau Mau terrorists and were detained.

> His hypocritical visions are exposed as sham and together with them he is shattered and broken. At the same time, he is cuckolded and despised by a forlorn and unfulfilled wife who has grown tired of playing a secondary role to his hollow ambitions.[18]

In *Weep Not, Child*, Ngugi does not give details about the detention camps. In *A Grain of Wheat* it is said that the White man's underlying energy, caught in senseless mass cruelty, is portrayed in detail. These were several detention camps spreading from the Manda islands in the Indian Ocean to the Magata islands in lake Victoria. Manda camp housed eighteen thousand people at a time. The suspected as well as the young men were caught and were sent to the detention camps. Their legs and hands were chained. The sanitary conditions were poor. Mugo said that at Rira camp, they were given 8.03 of meat per week and 7.03 of flour per day. Those who were attacked by typhoid were not given any treatment, when Robson was working as District officer at Rira camp.

John Thompson who had become popular while working at Yala camp on behalf of White government, was posted to Rira camp. He represented change in the attitude of the White government just before *Uhuru.* He changed the way of extracting secrets from the detainees. Earlier, it has been at Rira camp to bury a man naked in hot sand, sometimes leaving him there overnight. Thompson spoke with their detainees individually about homes and family members before trying to extract oaths from them. To extract the needed information from them, he told them that if they confessed they could join the family members and be happy. The hard cores got softened a little. In his attempts to extract information from the detainees at Rira camp, he even began to give treatment to those suffering from typhoid. When he was not able to make Mugo confess, he resorted to whipping him hard. Ngugi avoids excessive details in the description of such suppressive physical torture or pains inflicted on the detainees and concentrates on the psychological consequences of the atrocities. Mugo said:

> I saw men crawl on the ground . . . their hands and feet were chained with iron all the time. Now he spoke in a subjugated voice like a child. Once bottled necks were hammered in to people's backside and the men whimpered like caged animals, that last was at Rira. (208)

Besides delineating the untold suffering—physical and mental—of the people in detention camps, the novelist portrays the agonies of the people outside the camp. They are not allowed to give refuge to Mau Mau people. The remaining members of the family were forced to work on the fields of the White settlers and some to dig trenches. Those who did not work properly were beaten up. The following song rightly expresses the suffering and agony of the natives in the hands of the colonial government.

> The children of Israel,
> When they were in misery
> Were made to do work
> Harder than done by cow and donkeys. (164)

These lines of Mumbi throw light on 'the resurgence of new socialist awakening.' The novelist does not hesitate to comment on the ripples of hysteria that were spread during the Mau Mau rebellion. Everyone is under the grip of fear. The novelist picturesquely describes the psychological stress of the characters and their physical suffering during the emergency. The individual betrayals are also recorded. Mugo hands over Kihika, a Mau Mau patriot to the White government, when Kihika wants him to join the rebellion. Mugo expresses his fear thus: "If I work for him the government will catch me. The white man has long arms and they will hang me." (221)

The Whites dragged a few young people like Mugo and Gikonyo, and instilled fear to warn them not to act against the White government. Thus the fear induced by the Whites had far reaching effects on the Africans. At the detention camps, Mugo and Gikonyo lived under constant insecurity and fear. They were physically and mentally torn when they were back to their homes just before 'Uhuru.' Because of the effect of such prolonged psychological stress Gikonyo could not understand his wife in proper light. Insecure feeling continuously haunted Mugo.

The novelist also dwells upon the Whites before giving independence. They confiscated the lands of ever increasing number of detainees. Unfortunately, when the Africans went back from the detention camps, they were left without anything to live by. They could not even locate their houses for they were burnt and the whole of Thabai village itself was shifted to another place. Thus the White government confiscated Mugo's land on which he pinned hopes. The confiscated lands were sold to White settlers or the black people who were loyal to the White government.

Ngugi throws light on the group consciousness under exploitative conditions in his novels. In *A Grain of Wheat*, he doesn't fail to record the trauma of the villagers of Thabai and in *Petals of Blood*, he concentrates on Illmorog and the lives of its residents. In pre-colonial times, Illmorog was a purely traditional society untouched by western ways. The peasants reckoned their wealth in land, goats and cows. With the imperialistic intrusion, the decline of Illmorog began. Settlers, colonists and petty Indian traders exploited it. After 'Uhuru,' it was no more than it was ravished, abandoned ghost of its formal self. After the Europeans had left, African community was nothing but a tangle of disoriented isolated life. The economic exploitation of Kenya continued even after it attained independence in the form of foreign investments, international corporations and land occupations.

The White settlers exploited the peasants by imposing taxes on land. So, even the landowners suffered a lot at the hands of the Whites. The yield from their land dwindled. There were no common grassfields as in the past because the settlers occupied most of the fertile land. Ngunga's sons, unable to live on the limited lands they owned, turned into workers in European farms. One of them had become a cook in a European house. Ngunga felt sad that his grown-up sons had to use his hands for cooking in the Settler's home. The peasants after paying the taxes levied by the White rulers in the form of the cattle were reduced to a state of penury. The economic condition and the colonial exploitation of Illmorog had a devastating effect on the lives of the people who

> were unable to meet their demands. In the end they joined the very laboring clan they were trying to avoid by the sale of their lands and property. (90)

The severe drought hit Illmorog and its environs. There was neither shade nor rain as the Europeans carried away wood, charcoal from Illmorog forest to feed the machines and men. According to Munira.

> The railway line has eaten the forests; and after accomplishes their task the two sails were removed and the ground became a road—, a kind of road—that gave no evidence of its former exploitation glory. (11)

The forest wealth of Kenya has been taken away by the Whites. The Trans African road, linking Naircbi and Illmorog, had also connected many cities of the African continent. Every corner of the continent was now within the easy reach of international capitalists, robbery and exploitation. Through these roads Whites made profits selling their products such as guns, tractors, blades, and diesel engines. This curbed the iron-ore business in Africa. Ngugi focuses his attention on the economic exploitation of the Africans at the hands of the Whites.

This kind of economic exploitation of the Kenyans by the Europeans continued in the form of loans given by European banks and in the form of International companies owned by Europeans in neo-colonial Kenya. This economic exploitation continued even after Kenya attained independence with the help of bourgeoisie Africans. In *A Grain of Wheat*,

> He is concerned not merely with the wickedness of the oppressors, but with the weakness of the indigenous people themselves.[19]

The exploitation of the Africans by their fellow countrymen is examined in the next chapter.

NOTES

1. Ngugi wa Thiong'o, *Homecoming* (London: Heinemann, 1972), p. 50.
2. G.D. Killam, *An Introduction to the Writings of Ngugi wa Thiong'o* (London: Heinemann, 1980), p. 7.
3. C.B. Robson, *Ngugi wa Thiong'o* (London: Heinemann, 1979), p. 1.
4. Arthur Ravenscroft, *Ngugi wa Thiong'o, Contemporary Novelist*, ed. Lesley Henderson (London: Saint James Press, 1991), p. 695.
5. Ngugi wa Thiong'o, "Education for a National Culture," *UFA-HAMU*, Vol. XII, No. 2 (1983), p. 24.
6. Ngugi, *Homecoming*, p. 31.
7. Robson, p. 8.
8. Jagdish Rai, "The Wounded Psyche of Africa as Reflected in Achebe's *Arrow of God*, Palmer's *Turbottwolf* and Ngugi's *The River Between*," *Commonwealth Fiction* (New Delhi: Classical, 1988), Vol. 3, p. 122.
9. Chinua Achebe, *Things Fall Apart* (London: Heinemann, 1958), p. 158.
10. Werner Glinga, "*The River Between* and its Forerunners: A Contribution to the Theory of Kenyan Novel," *WLWE*, Vol. 26, No. 2 (1986) p. 213.
11. T.N. Dhar, "Private Dreams and Public Pressures: Ngugi wa Thiong'o's *Weep Not, Child* and *River Between*," *Commonwealth Fiction* (New Delhi: Classical, 1988), Vol. 3, p. 235.
12. Ngugi, "Education," p. 24.
13. Jomo Kenyetta, *Facing Mount Kenya* (London: Martin Secker and Warburg, 1938), p. 21.
14. Magina Magina Interviews Ngugi wa Thiong'o, *African Report*, No. 90 (Feb. 1979), pp. 30-31.
15. Bette J. Parker, BBB Interviews Ngugi wa Thiong'o, *Blacks Books Bulletin*, Vol. 6. No. 1 (Spring, 1978), p. 51.

16. David Cook, *Ngugi wa Thiong'o: An Exploration of His Writings* (London: Heinemann, 1983), p. 72.
17. Ime Ikeidden, "James Ngugi as a Novelist," *African Literature Today*, No. 2 (1969), p. 10.
18. Cook, p. 72.
19. Eustace Palmer, *An Introduction to the African Novel* (London: Heinemann, 1972), p. 26.

Chapter 4

Exploitation of the Africans by the Africans

As a creative Process, fiction is an expression of the most intimate awareness of the society in which it is born and in which it evolves. Small wonder therefore, if the evolution of fiction and the evolution of the consciousness of social apparatus are simultaneous and interlocked. African fiction has had inextricable links with the socio-political milieu. The African novelist sought to explore and interpret Africans significantly in its various aspects—social, political, economic and cultural. Ngugi artistically expressed the urges and aspirations of the people who were heroically involved in the struggle for equality and justice. In his works, besides depicting a deep sense of African deprivation and of the desire to win back a lost heritage, he convincingly and effectively records "the lives of dispossessed little people that are all broken by an imported capitalist system."[1] With greater fervour and rhetoric, he renews his attack on the neo-colonial exploiters of ordinary Kenyans in various spheres of social life.

In *The River Between*, Ngugi records the traditions and customs of the people of Kenya. Kameno, Mykuyu and Honia River form a pattern of ridge and a valley that is still a major characteristic of the Gikuyu area of Kenya. This Gikuyu land is a land of great fertility and promise. The people maintain the tribe's magic and rituals pure and intact. Ngugi makes custom of circumcision the centre of the novel and describes how the early African converts into the new faith of Europeans indulged in the cultural exploitation of their fellow Kenyans.

It was the time when Europeans came with their religion and settled at Siriana, a place near Mykuyu and Kameno ridges. Joshua and Kabonyi were converted to the new faith along with few others on the ridges. Joshua feared the revenge of his friends as he betrayed them by converting into new faith. But at Siriana,

> he found a sanctuary and the White man's power and magic. . . . The new faith worked in him till it came to possess him wholly. He renounced his tribal magic power and ritual. He turned to and felt deep presence of the one God. (29)

He preached in sharp ringing tones the presence of that one God—the White man's God. He believed like Livingstone of Siriana mission that Gikuyu God is the 'prince of darkness' and Africans, the 'children of darkness.' He thought that by getting baptised, he has become a new creature who escaped the hell. He no longer feared Chege, the tribal leader of the ridges. He, as an agent of Siriana mission, preached with vehemence and spoke of White man's power and knowledge and converted a few Africans to follow new faith abandoning the traditional customs. Joshua, born on that land, began to condemn the land's ways more vehemently than the White man. Thus he became a powerful and direct cultural exploiter of the Africans.

Joshua also aided the White men to advance further into the land with his new ways. People of Kameno blamed Joshua who interfered in the matter of taxes levied on them by the White government. To the people on the ridge, taxes were new. They could not understand them. But Joshua, who knew about them all, felt that it was his duty to obey the White government. He wanted to force the people on to their knees to follow the ways of the White man. He prayed god thus:

> Bring down fire and thunder
> Bring down the flood. (32)

He forced even his family members to follow his new ways strictly. He got circumcised while he was young and married circumcised Miriam, but after converting into new faith, he felt that it was an unforgivable sin to follow the ritual of circumcision. Unable to follow his religion, which has no relevance to the people living there, his two daughters, broke away from him. His new belief, which has neither understanding nor forgiveness, was not able to hold back his family from disintegration. Chege comments on the popular feelings thus:

> You see what discord in the family does. If Joshua has not sold his heart to these people, it would have been a simple case. (48)

Led by Joshua and Kabonyi, Mykuyu became the land of Christians, while Kameno still followed the old customs. Chege has seen more than any one else that:

> Kabonyi and Joshua . . . would not come to any good. . . . These followers of Joshua would bring so many divisions to land that the tribe would die. (37)

Joshua's preaching indeed divided the people who followed the new faith and the people who followed the old faith. As the differences grew, the Christian people of Makuyu stopped to have terms with the traditional people of Kameno. Naturally, he incurred the anger of the people who lit fire to the huts as "an expression of that widened gulf." (141)

> Joshua was identified as the enemy of the tribe. He was with Siriana, with the White settlers. For now it was said that Siriana missionaries had been sent to prepare the way for the settlers. (110)

Joshua who renounced his life-giving traditions of the tribe had no roots to stand upon and grow. He, therefore, clinged to missionaries, which promised future to him, and became the exploiter of his own race.

Thus Joshua, though born on Kenyan land, involved in direct cultural exploitation of the Kenyans. The way, which he and his followers eased for the Europeans, later led to drastic effects on the lives of the Kenyans. The Whites began to pour into the interiors in greater number. He aided the White government in its political advancement and in its economic exploitation of the natives.

Kabonyi who joined the Europeans, along with Joshua to buy African souls through their religion to them, could not become a popular leader like Joshua. Aiming to become popular like Joshua on the ridges, Kabonyi led a breakaway movement from Joshua and his followers. 'Kiama' movement, which he led, aimed to uphold the traditions and customs of the ridges. Though he did not believe in its principles, he exploited the inclination of majority of the people living on the ridges at the right time to become powerful and popular. But Waiyaki was growing more popular as the 'teacher' and 'saviour' of the ridges. Kabonyi who wanted his son Kamau to become the most popular figure on the ridges could not tolerate this and grew jealous of him. Kamau wanted to marry Joshua's daughter, Nyambura. But Nyambura and Waiyaki were in love with each other. Both father and son planned the doom of Waiyaki through 'Kiama' and led the people against them. According to 'Kiama' principles, Waiyaki who took the oath of 'Kiama' cannot marry uncircumcised Nyambura. Even Kamau could not marry her according to the movement's principles. But he and his father made Waiyaki a prey to their jealousy. Death was the punishment for those who violated the oath. Thus Kabonyi hindered the growth of a leader on the ridges. He as a convert was a cultural exploiter of the Africans. In fact, he evolved as an opportunist and exploiter of his fellow Africans in the novel.

While Joshua and Kabonyi involved in the exploitation of the Africans directly and knowingly, Chege and his son Waiyaki were also exploiters indirectly without their knowledge. Chege exposed his son to the White man's education and religion by sending him to Siriana missionary school. His son, Waiyaki, became 'soft.' The uneasiness in the mind of Waiyaki regarding the circumcision revealed his non-acceptance of the tribal customs. It was said, "even Waiyaki was slightly embarrassed" (56). This in a way was an expression of the suppression of his native tribal belief.

Waiyaki in an attempt to quench the growing thirst of education among the people of the ridges opens as many schools as possible. He even brought teachers from Siriana mission. Thus he indulged in exploitation by establishing the foundation of White man's education. Rightly does he aid "the penetration of the long arm of the White man by spreading his culture and by using teachers from outside the ridges."[2]

Schools grew like mushrooms on the ridges. Without his knowledge Waiyaki directed the peoples' attention in the wrong route. At that time he should have taught 'unity' to the people to drive away the Whites from occupying their land, he thwarted their interest. Jomo Kenyatta puts Waiyaki's innovations into perspective:

> Apart from the system of schools, which has been introduced by the Europeans, there is no special school building in the Gikuyu sense of the word. The homestead is a school.[3]

In *Weep Not, Child*, Ngugi records the exploitation of the Africans at the hands of the African landlords. Jacobo, who is nicknamed 'black European' indulges in ruthless exploitation of the African farmers. His political allegiance, his house and his privileged positions set him apart from most of his countrymen. He hindered other farmers from growing rich like him. His land was as big as a settler's farm.

> Jacobo was lucky because he had for many years been the only African allowed to grow pyrethrum . . . he had stood in the way of similar permits being given to other people. (45)

In return to the permission given by the settlers to grow cash crops, Jacobo recruited labour and gave Howlands advice on how to get hard work from African workers for unfair wages. Ngotho, as one of the workers supplied by him to Howlands, suffered in the suppressive hands of Jacobo. Jacobo acted as an agent to the Whites in pacifying the Africans to work for low wages. He was raised to a chief's position on account of his suppressive power. Acting as an agent to Howlands, he tried in vain to pacify the revolted Ngotho. Unsuccessful in his attempt, he becomes an opponent to Ngotho and nurses deep-seated resentment against him. He searches continually for ways of getting Ngotho and his sons out of the way to win Howlands's favour. He tells Howlands:

> Now, if we leave them alone, there'll flare up big, big trouble in the village. Their detention would make it easier to keep an eye on this Ngotho because as I was telling you he may be the real leader of Mau Mau. (89)

These lines throw light on the exploitative nature of Jacobo. Even Howlands despised Jacobo 'because he was a savage.'

A Grain of Wheat is about the Mau Mau independence war. It also keeps flashing back to individual suffering in Mau Mau days. It lays bare on the new African politicians betraying the ordinary people who suffered under colonialism.

> The food that which sowest is not quickened, expect it die. And that which thou sowest, thou sowest not that body that shall be, but bare grain, it may be a chance of wheat, or of some other grain.[4]

This epigraph acquires significance in the context of the theme of exploitation in the novel. In this novel, one finds exploitation of the Africans at the hands of the fellow Africans. The novelist feels that "the soil and sense of community provided by the ridges is strongly conveyed."[5]

Mugo indulges in exploitation as he ignores his responsibility to his group. He is haunted because he escapes from his responsibility to the group and to the nation.

In the African context, a selfish person was nicknamed '*Mwenbongia*' and he doesn't have any name or reputation in society. He is looked at with suspicion and as one who is likely to end up his life as a wizard. The novelist depicts the clashes between the individual aspirations and tribal or group feelings. Mugo in the novel decides to betray Kihika, a patriot who participated actively in the Mau Mau revolution. Mugo's betrayal is logical outcome of personal development. His betrayal is induced by his jealousy and partly he wants not to be drawn unnecessarily in connection with others. In his own words:

> I wanted to live my life. I never wanted to be involved in anything. Then he came into my life, here, a night like this and pulled me into the stream. So I killed him. (161)

Mugo does not hesitate to betray Kihika, when he takes refuge in Mugo's hut. Mugo serves as a Judas figure. He walks to D.O office and informs the Whites about Kihika's whereabouts. He remembers how Isaq and Moses were saved from death. He says:

> I am important. I must not die. To keep myself alive, healthy, strong—to wait for mission in life—is a duty to myself, to men and women of tomorrow. (223)

Ngugi projects Mugo as Judas who betrayed Jesus Christ.

Karanja, chief of the homeguards, too indulges in ruthless exploitation. He represents the mentality of colonised African as exactly as Kihika represents the opposite. He becomes a trustworthy lieutenant of the White man, first as a homeguard and later as the chief during the emergency. The novelist repugnantly depicts his betrayal of the Africans.

On Sunday, at the railway station, he came out candidly that he should ignore the indifferent behaviour of his fellowmen and promote his own interest. He says:

> The Earth was going around again I must run he thought it cannot be helped. Why should I fear to trample on the children, the lame and the weak when others are doing it. (82)

Consistence with this perception, he aligns himself with the Europeans. He is not prepared to even go as far as Gikonyo in service to the cause. His youthful contempt for Kihika together with his sense of self-preservation makes him a black exploiter. Naturally, his own people distrust him most. Karanja is so dismal that he does not hesitate to betray his friend Gikonyo. The two have been friendly, warm since their childhood. By ignoring the intimacy he has had with Gikonyo, he indulges in the 'unheroic' act of seducing Mumbi, Gikonyo's wife. Gikonyo who comes to know about the betrayal comments on Karanja thus: "I suppose there is nothing so painful as finding that a friend, or a man you always trusted, has betrayed you." (122)

Ngugi, by employing the method of parallels and contrasts, points out that "Independence marks the end of one's struggle, it is also the beginning of another."[6]

One notices this in the exploitation made by an M.P. who misleads Gikonyo. Here, the M.P. replaces Mr. Burton and also becomes a member of a new aristocracy. Gikonyo rightly observes that the people who did not take part in the freedom richly reaped the fruits. He says:

> It is people like you who ought to have been the first to taste the fruits of independence. But now, whom do we see riding along in cars and changing them as if motor cars were clothes. It is those who did not take in movement, the same who ran to shelter of schools, and universities and administration. (80)

Lack of values signifies the post-Independence Gikuyu community. Gikonyo was an artisan prior to independence. After the independence, he indulges in economic exploitation by moving into the world of women's market trading. The novelist "transfers a previous cultural hero from his former position to that of the new cultural hero based on post-emergency values. This activity is presented as being neither healthy nor necessarily admirable."[7] These lines throw light on Gikonyo who comes before us a Neo-European exploiting his own people.

Ngugi focuses his attention on 'Thabi Village' with burnt houses and people without proper food and shelter. Selfish and greedy African people were used by the White government as homeguards. The Africans were set against the other Africans. Those who worked as agents to the Whites were promoted depending on their capacity to suppress and inflict pain on their fellow Africans. Thus Karanja was promoted as the chief of the homeguards. The White government countenanced the immoral acts of homeguards that picked women and molested them.

Thus in *A Grain of Wheat*, individual betrayals become the representative of the vast betrayal of the whole society. The leaders of Kenya at the time of 'Uhuru' indulged in exploitation and became "a tribe of operators and manipulators who in their own narrow interest replaced colonialism with neocolonialism."[8]

This novel thus becomes not simply a social document but a social force. These feelings of exploitation of the Africans are further exemplified in Ngugi's another powerful novel, *Petals of Blood.*

Ngugi added artistic representation of the betrayal of independence movement and its authors, the nature of cost of modernity as it coincides with the emergence of a Kenyan middle class and of the need for the creation of "a cultural liberation struggle fostered by peasants and workers."[9]

Illmorog becomes a living presence in the novel. It is in the grip of prolonged drought. Even the M.P. has conveniently ignored the village. So the desperate villagers take an epic march to the capital to lay their troubles before the authorities. Subsequently religious, political and economic exploiters swarm upon Illmorog and exploit it by using such devices as for closed loans and dispose the local inhabitants. Thus the novelist conveys "a ruthless tripping of already deprived ordinary people."[10]

Ngugi is very unhappy for he feels that independent movement has been betrayed, as the peasant and the worker, for whom the war was fought, have been further alienated from the land which is the source of life. He is of the opinion that the poor or the drooped are made pitiable by the growing Kenyan middle class, entrepreneurs in league with international finance capitalism. The confiscation of Kenyan lands by the Europeans had a far-reaching effect on the Kenyan people even after Kenya attained independence. Karega's family lived as squatters on different Europeans' farms providing free labour in return for some grazing and cultivation on the settler's land. They were given a particular piece of land in the bush to get it ready for the European landlord to cultivate. After a year they were driven off and were shown other virgin land to clear. This process went on and on. They paid the taxes in the form of goats. Miriam continued to live life as a squatter while her youngest educated son, Karega, on whom she had pinned her hopes, spent all his life in an attempt to make his living and in trying to set things right in neocolonial Kenya, after it was ravished during the colonial time. At the end of the novel, he realised his failure:

> What of all the Miriamus of Kenya, of neo-colonial Africa? What of all the women and men and children still weighed down by imperialism. (342)

The lines show how Africans have been alienated from their land first by the colonialists and later by a class of African landlords.

Even after Kenya attained independence, the business field was dominated by Europeans who provided the local directorships to the Kenyan ministers and others in high positions who exploited wealth of Kenya. Fine example is Thengeta Breweries. Wanja and Abdulla were responsible for popularising Thengeta Breweries as a drink in Illmorog. But they could not compete with larger concerns, which control the economy there. The license for brewing Thengeta by Abdulla and Wanja was cancelled by corrupt officials like Cheri. Mzigo and Kimero became the shareholders and directors of the new Thengeta Breweries. But the company was owned by an Anglo-American international company. Thengeta drink brewed from Thengeta plant, which grew wild on the plains, was associated in pre-colonial times with vitality and vigour. In neo-colonial Kenya it was made into a spirit drink and it demoralised the Kenyans. It was consumed only on festival occasions in the past and was believed to have medicinal value. But now, it is consumed as a hot drink. The transformation of Thengeta into a debased modern spirit by the capitalists suggest the erosion of traditional valves and destruction of traditional innocence by the corrupt and the deprived agency of modernism.

The novelist does not hesitate to delineate the exploitation of the Africans at the hands of the politicians. After the independence, the Kenyans repose trust and confidence in their representatives. When Illmorog is affected by drought, they approach Nderi, their M.P., for help. But unfortunately, the M.P. does not extend any help to the villagers and asks them mercilessly:

> Now, I want you to go back to Illmorog. Get yourselves together. Subscribe money. You can even sell some of the cows and goats instead of letting them die. Dive deep into your pockets. (*PB*, 182)

This shows that the politicians could not rise above their petty nature in helping the Kenyans.

One notices the impact of cultural imperialism and the exploitation of the Africans in their own society. This can be illustrated from the love between Karega and Mukum. Mukum's father drew his daughter to suicide because he thought respectable families like his could not countenance an alliance with a family like Karega. Karega's brother Ndinga was believed to have deprived brother Ezekiel of his right ear as a punishment for preaching against the Mau Mau movement in church. Wanja's father could not allow making friendship with a boy whose family was poor and irreligious. Juliana in *Weep Not, Child* never allowed her children to mix with other 'primitive children.' The cultural imperialism blinded these Africans and as a result their children became victims of their narrow, snobbish religious beliefs. The rich Africans also followed colour bar introduced by the colonists.

Even after independence, the Kenyans became a prey to the exploitation at the hands of fellow Kenyans. The Whites continued to own big hotels, industries and factories in Nairobi. They gave petty jobs to the Kenyans. Illmorog was depopulated. Only the old people and children lived there. The young men occasionally visited the place and 'bellied the women' left behind. There were none to improve the conditions of Illmorog. The economic conditions of the young men did not permit them to take their folk to the cities where they worked. The children were not cared for. Such of those who were averse to work on the farms of the Whites had to sell away their lands and other property to keep going. "In the end, they joined the very labouring class they were trying to avoid by the sale of their land property." (90)

Ngugi successfully delineates the theme of exploitation by employing the road image in the novel. In the beginning when Munira arrives in Illmorog, there is only a dirt road which is described as "being as treacherous as those hags and brags and cripples." (11) In part IV, it has become the Trans-Africa road, heavy with tankers linking Nairobi to Illmorog. The destruction of the pastoral street is very well indicated by arrival of new road. Ironically, the Africans are brought closer together in one way, but estranged in another. As the author comments:

> the road was built, not to give content and reality to the vision of a continent, but to show our readiness and . . . every corner of the

> continent was now within the reach of international capitalist robbery and exploitation. (262)

This only shows that the plundering of Africa by the previous generations of profiteers is now to be followed by an exploitation of the continent by itself.

The novelist gives the desolate conditions that prevail in Illmorog during the neo-colonial times. New constructions take place in Illmorog overnight. It becomes famous:

> Well-beyond the walls of ridge and plains. The feverish growth of the city witnesses a church, a police station and a distillery. The peasants are reduced into easy bank loans and find their lands taken from them.[11]

Utamaduni, a cultural tourist centre is created not only attracting the tourist and getting dollars from them but in reality to serve as a centre for:

> smuggling gemstones and ivory plus animal and even human skins. It was a centre for the plunder of the country's natural and human assets. (334)

Land becomes the most central to the novels, as the novelist earnestly feels that the Africans have been alienated from the land first by the colonialist and next by the imperial colonialists. The imperial colonists helped themselves to the land paying into the pockets of a few whatever worth they consigned to it and subsequently by a class of landlords who because of their connections with the forces of world capitalism, are able to manage the purchase prize. The problems of the Kenyans are to re-achieve the land. The struggle has a neo-colonial dimension. The novelist says:

> Within only ten years . . . Illmorog peasants had been displaced from the land: some had joined the army of workers. Others were semi-workers with one foot in a plot of land and one foot in a factory. (302)

Nyakinyua, Wanja's grandmother, finds fault with the fellow Africans:

> I'll go alone . . . my man fought the white man. He paid for it with his blood. . . . I'll struggle against these black oppressors . . . alone. (276)

Regarding religion, the novelist has a grumble. He deplores the historical brand of evangelicalism practised by Munira in part III of the novel. He also becomes critical of the formal Christian religion. Both forms of Christianity divert people's attention from contemplating the real nature of the circumstance and what they must do to correct these. So he opposes Munira's father's religion that supports the oppressor.

In the realm of religion one notices certain elements of exploitation. The Christian religion, which has a firm hold over the lives of the people, is presented here as oppressive, unsympathetic and hypocritical. Munira's father who is a Church person as well as the pillar of the state is really a capitalist and a black slaver of the most rapid sort. He is an opportunist who in his younger days turned his back on his traditional society and joined the White man and also supported the White oppressors against the Mau Mau freedom fighters. Now, he participates actively in sordid exploitation of the masses. His religion is a life-denying force, which has stifled the life in Munira's wife and children. He is an irreligious man who cannot see that his Christians should preclude the taking of an oath geared towards the consolidation of tribalism. He even holds the opinions that God would throw his weight behind such a move. He is insensitive to what obtains in society. The narrator rightly observes and comments on the opportunistic, hypocritical and exploitative nature of Ezekiel, another religious nature in the novel. He is a respected elder in the hierarchy of Presbyterian Church.

> He was tall and mean in his holiness. . . . He was . . . especially successful in attracting faithful labour on his farm. . . . There were . . . some who . . . demand higher wages . . . they would be dismissed. (14)

Thus he never practised the tenets of Christianity but indulged in exploitation of poor workers.

The novelist does not hesitate to discuss the field and the exploitative and irrelevant measures that obtain even during the neo-colonial period. This is illustrated from the school at Siriana. Chui and Munira have been schoolboys together at Siriana. Chui leads a strike against Fraudsham, the head master of the school and sees to it that the latter is sent to overseas to complete his education there. Karega in the succeeding generation leads a strike against Fraudsham. Naturally, the strike becomes fruitful with deposition of the Fraudsham and the succession of Chui as the headmaster. Karega and his classmates anticipate a new beginning, a reform of the curriculum, ultimately new people. Unfortunately, Chui a black replica of Fraudsham, continues the outworn tradition of alien culture at the school.

For Chui this is only a first step on the road to become an investor in the foreign exploitation of his country. Karega feels that he must come through education to ameliorate the life of the exploitative masses.

In the realm of education also, one perceives a note of disillusionment because the system is in tune with the political reality of Kenya. The purpose and content of imperialist education is thoroughly scrutinised and its relevance to the African situation is questioned. In the words of Palmer:

> It is projected as an oppressive, irrelevant and racialist system obviously geared towards the perpetuating of White man's domination and instilling into people's respect for British institution and attitudes.[12]

Fraudsham is an embodiment of the educational process in Kenya. His successor Chui, an African, in his student days has been victimised by the oppressive imperialistic system of education. So Chui, who might have effected changes, unfortunately turns out to be more European in his attitude than Fraudsham himself. When Karega and his revolutionary contemporaries organise strike, first against the White Fraudsham, then against the Black Chui, they demand an African content to the education Africans are being given. They demand that African Literature and African History must be taught in schools to know about themselves and their environment. They become critical of an educational system that teaches them about White snow, spring flowers, fluttering by icy lakes. As the African ethos has not been incorporated in the system, the Kenyans feel that they are being exploited.

The behaviour of the Revs. Kaman and Jerrod reinforces this impression of religious bankruptcy. Jerrod would like to lead a sermon to starving people about the need for industry and delays medical attention to a sick boy.

Where Illmorog attains prosperity, Jerrod becomes a sort of society clergyman, the vicar of the most fashionable church in the neighbourhood. The church is a great proprietor, its priests being no different from other modern black capitalists and imperialists. The exploitation of the capitalists is grippingly described in the novel. As they move in with their lands, factories, distillieries, estate agencies, the old and traditional Illmorog is immensely destroyed. The novelist gives a good account of bewildered and deceased peasants unable to match the business acumen and financially standing big men from the city. Inevitably, they lose their land and all their positions and degenerate helplessly into labourers. It is only Nyakinyua who puts up the determined fight against the forces that have deprived her of her heritage. Her determination constitutes the last flagging attempt to save a once dignified and secure society. To resist the encroachment of the new men, unfortunately, it is doomed to failure because of the reluctance of others to support her. It is transformed into a capitalist society with all the attendant problems of prostitution, social inequality and inadequate housing for the poor. Palmer comments: "It has twice been exploited and destroyed, once by the White imperialist and now by their successors the black imperialist." (294)

In the political area also, corruption and exploitation have crept in. One sees a representative of politician in M.P. who is incompetent, corrupt and indifferent to the sufferings of the people. Like other politicians, he converts the money, he has collected from his constituency for a water project, into security for loans, buying shares in companies and investing in lands, housing and small business. He has become one of the country's capitalists. He is one who has thrived on the politics. Even the political party becomes notorious because of its corruption, thuggery and indifference to the people's plight. The politicians in Kenya indulge in exploitation by remaining blind to the real problems like poverty, starvation, and inadequate housing and educational provision. They became rich, fat and live in palatial buildings in the cities.

The novelist spares no pains in exposing the traitors who prosper after independence. Kimeria, Mzigo, Chui and Nderi ride on Mercedes Benzes, own thousands of acres of land and housing estates. They also own Breweries, visit expensive night-clubs and exploit women. The corruption of the system results in the under-utilisation and destruction of potential in Kenya. Karega rightly comments:

> How now, how could the young, the bright and the helpful deteriorate so? What there is no way of using their energies and dreams to a higher purpose than the bottle, the jute box and sickness on a cement floor? (103)

The symbol of petals of blood as in the poem by Derek Walcott suggests destruction, evil, the unnatural, corruption and death. Usually, the petals here are connected with the potent ginger lily, one of the destructive, repulsive plants which give normally quite natural and beautiful look but an eerie unnatural and evil aura. The symbol suggests the distortion of things in this society from the normal and natural to the abnormal and evil and the introduction of chaos and destruction where there should be beauty and order. In the novel itself, we come to know that the flower with petals of blood belongs to a plant that grows wild in the plains. One child cries out thus:

> 'Look. A flower with petals of blood.'
>
> It was a solitary red bean flower in a field dominated by blue, white and violet flowers. 'No matter how you looked at it, it gave you the impression of the flow of blood . . . this is a worm-eaten flower. . . . It cannot bear fruit. That's why we must kill worms. . .

> . A flower can also become this colour if it is prevented reaching the light.' (21-22)

Unlike the flower in the prefix, the flower with the Petals of Blood is itself the victim of evil; the agents of corruption have destroyed its innocence. The blood suggests suffering. The flower becomes a symbol of the Kenyan society. Ngugi is concerned with potential, beautiful and productive but its potential unrealised and itself destroyed by the agents of corruption and death.

Thus *Petals of Blood* is an angry novel recording various facets of exploitation in Kenyan society. With greater fervour of feeling and rhetoric, Ngugi renews the neo-colonial exploitation of ordinary Kenyan people in his next novel, *Devil on the Cross*.

With a view to reaching the larger number of people, he wrote in Gikuyu. In his own words:

> Free thoughts on toilet papers! I had deliberately given myself to difficult task . . . the Kenyan people's struggles against the neo-colonial form and stage of imperialism.[13]

The novelist is worried about corruption that is rampant in the Kenyan society. He feels that capitalism is a systematic robbery of peasants and workers. A robbery protected and sanctified by large courts, parliament, religion, armed forces, police and educational institutions. In fact, he doesn't hesitate to exhibit bolder strokes in this novel. By arousing the predicament of the oppressed, he propels them into combined action to set right the situation. One is reminded of Swift's *Gulliver's Travels*. Fielding's *The Life of Jonathan Wild*, Pope's *Dunciad* and Orwell's *Animal Farm*.

The novel opens at a crush in a realistic society. Then there is a journey in a taxi from Nairobi to Illmorog during which the driver and five passengers discuss social issues, which are most central to the novel. Their narration of their experiences is punctuated by the flashes of satanical absurdity. The various invitation cards to the Devil's Feast in Illmorog are scrutinised. After we have been informed of intentions of the travellers in the taxi to attend the gathering in Illmorog, the scene in the minibus, simply melts into the voice of the meetings of the masters of ceremonies:

> And now, before I sit down, I shall call upon the leaders of foreign delegation from the international organisation thieves and robbers whose headquarters are in New York, U.S.A. to talk to you. I think you all know that we have already applied to become full members of IOTR. Their visit to this delegation thus, the gifts and the crown they have brought marks the beginning of even more fruitful period of co-operation.[14]

The seven representatives are the neo-colonial powers indulging in the most heinous corrupt practices and exploitation. Each one wears shirts made of paper money of their respective homelands and reveals his grabbing of the Kenyan economy. They take away the natural resources of Kenyans and also indulge in exploitation of the workers and peasants. Gitutu is a big-bellied person who fattens on land. He proudly relates how he has taken over vast estates from White settlers, subdivided them into plots and sold them at high prices to citizens. He says frankly:

> The land wasn't mine and the money with which I had paid for wasn't mine and I hadn't added anything to the land where did I get the 2,20,000 shilling? From the pockets of the people. Yes, because the land really belonged to people, and the money with which I bought it came from the people. (106)

This passage exhibits the grabbing of the lands of the poor peasants by the black imperialists like Gitutu Kihaahu. The land key adulterous detonates his practices of exploitation in three areas, viz., education, local government and housing. In education he has discovered a method of luring the status secrets to his school. He does not approve of any indigenous syllabus in his school curriculum. The advertisement in newspaper ran thus:

> Modern-Day Nursery School.
> Experienced European Principal.
> Formerly for Europeans Only,
> Now Open to a Few Kenyans.
> Foreign Standards as Before.
> National Languages, National Songs, National Names Banned.

> Foreign Languages, Foreign Songs, Foreign Toys etc., etc.
> English Medium of Instruction
> Limited Places.
> Telephone or Call in Your Car
> Colour is no Bar: Money is the Bar
> Fees High. (113)

In the local elections, Kinaa Ku indulges in corrupt practices. He bribes the voter, indulges in rigging and wins the elections. He easily becomes the chairman of local housing committee. He does not hesitate to get percentages by foreign speculators in exchange for building contracts and then corruptly allocates the Jerry built Maisonettes that result to join in his pocket even more money. The community ensures debased local administration while publicly subsidised housing is hawked on a black market.

Ngugi does not hesitate to depict the confrontation that flares up the pot-bellied and the cadaverous exploiters. The fat persons indulge in unscrupulous commercialism and there is a discussion on the topic that elite should exploit only the poor. There are references to adulterous false educators and business tycoons. One of the exploiters comments:

> I hadn't shed a drop of sweat. All my money came. . . . I never stopped plucking it. I picked one fruit after another. The sweet juice would spill out the corners of my mouth before I learned to eat more decrepitly. (116)

Nditika takes up another area of exploitation, namely the practice of smuggling—cornering goods and hiking up prices of essential commodities through black market. The whole narration runs like a treatise on exploitation of the Africans by the African imperialists.

Mwireri demands that exploitation be made exclusively indigenous, cut free from foreigners who take the richest pickings. He reveals how the multinationals force the local enterprise out of the market by under-selling cooking oil, skin lighteners or contraceptives. Mwireri is killed for questioning the neo-colonial basis of exploitation.

The novel reaches its peak when each speaker claims the crown of social crime and gives a brand new scheme of exploitation. Kihaaku describes the plastic puppets of White children he deploys to supplement White head ministers in entitling parents to send their children to schools. Gituku looks forward to the class when instead of tiny toys, plots of land being sold, citizens will queue up to buy near plots or trays of soil to grow for sustenance. He would also sell the air to the workers in airtight bottles. Kihaaku forecasts a time when it would be peddled to the works folds but the tiny portable tents or birds' nests that they pitch like nomads to shelter their heads while bodies remain at the mercy of the elements. Nditika suggests in conferring the market in the human organs for transplants so that the elite will purchase the physical immortality and leave death to others.

Kimeenderi caps all that has gone before. He outlines his plan to head all workers into barbed wire compounds where their blood split will be thumped, squeezed and dripped from them daily and sent out packaged by pipe lines to the home or kept for export while the donors are kept quiescent by means of conditioned religion, education and pseudo-culture. The forces of law and repression will be kept in reverse in the background. He also insists that the Christian mass has already pointed the way to Kimeederi's ideal by urging the regular imbedding of Christ's flesh and blood, a last twist of knife, which may have many leaders crying out in protest together with Wariinga herself.

The feast at the cave is the reunion of the former colonial masters represented by the people, the multi-national companies and the Kenyan ruling elite represented by their businessmen. The testimonies are the rendering of an account by the latter to the former in respect of the talents, which were to be looked after. The novel artistically renders how the Kenyan bourgeois elite exploited an army of workers, peasants, petty traders and students. The Kenyan capitalists are described as the thieves, robbers, hypocrites and criminals. To put it in a nutshell, "fantasy in this novel is only the gateway to realism."[15]

It is pertinent to note a few events of realism in the novel. The novel records how the African multi-millionaires made money by indulging in the exploitation of the Africans. The trademark bulging belly, the arrogance of power, the uncurbed ambition and cynicism characterising African imperialist stooges in their pursuit of wealth are all sad facts of life in today's African society. The acute feeling in the cave created by the fantastic testimonies is judiciously interrupted and replaced by a feeling of tangible reality achieved through technical break in the plot and an emphasis on the ordinary details of life. Religious hypocrisy, socio-political corruption, the brutal sexual and material exploitation suffered by the Kenyans at the hands of their bourgeoisie are very well depicted in the novel.

Ngugi would like to show that exploiters would go to any extent to promote their interest. They have a desire to make money at the cost of moral scruples. It is due to their materialistic interest that they sold their motherland to the colonisers. It is for the same reason that they continue to serve it into neo-colonialism. Colonialism, later neo-colonialism, helped to statue the characters' narrow, selfish and greedy appetites. In this novel individual appetites were absorbed into the collective inspirations in communal ideals.

There are a few references to religion in the novel. Mwireri assures his fellow passengers that majority of those who will be attending the feast believe in God. He says, "I for instance go to P.Cea at Thogoto, the Church of the Torch every Sunday" (76). The hell's angels lead the assemblage in the cave in signalling as if they were in Church: "Good news has come. To our country good news has come about our saviours." (90) Christianity does not serve any purpose. So he says:

> if you prevented people from breathing, what would prevent from taking up clubs and swords and guns. Better meanness that is convert; better a system of theft that is disguised by lies. Or why do you think that our imperialist friend brought us the Bible? Do you think that they were being foolish when they urged workers and peasants to close their eyes in prayer and told them earthling things were vain? Why do you think I go to all the Church fund-raising Haraambee meetings. (123)

Through the use of songs, Ngugi discusses contemporary issues and also the element of exploitation by the Africans. For example, Gatuiria sings thus:

> Hail, our land!
> Hail, Mount Kenya!
> Hail, our land,
> Never without water or food or green fields!

Wariinga also sings thus:

> Hail, the splendour of this land!
> Hail, the land ringed with deep lakes. (128)

Wangari and Muthuri also burst out into song thus:

> Famine has increased in our land
> But it has been given other name.
> So that the people should not discover
> Where all the food has been hidden. (150)

Through the use of songs, the novelist reiterates the theme of exploitation of the Africans at the hands of the fellow Africans.

Thus in *Devil on the Cross*, Ngugi says that the Devil is worshipped by the capitalist power magnets. It is Satan who exposes the precise methods of power of the elite and their cynical exploitation of the religion. Satan made a true picture of what was going on in the neo-colonial Kenya. The pattern of exploitation reaches its zenith:

> We, who are gathered here now, belong to one clan: the clan of workers--I think all of us saw the incredible spectacle of those who have bellies that never bear children come to scorn us. Those bellies are not swollen by disease. They have been fattened by the fruit of our sweat and blood. Those bellies are barren and their owners are barren. What about us the workers? . . . Today here, we refuse to go on being the pot that cooks but never tastes the food. (208)

Here, Ngugi through the image of cooking shows that the cook, in spite of his tasty food, is deprived of eating it as he is not allowed to eat the pudding by the master of the house. Similarly, the peasants and the workers in Kenyan society toil and produce resources which are never enjoyed by them. It is due to the exploitation of the neo-colonial Africans who exploit the poor and the indigent.

This theme of exploitation of Africans by the Africans recurs in his powerful novel, *Matigari*. Matigari has the following genesis. The word 'Matigari' seems to have emerged from its etymological and generic use as a reference to the leftovers of food or dregs in drinks to become a signifier of Mau Mau and to function on a higher discursive level as troop mediating the colonial past and the postcolonial movement. At this time, Matigari represented an attempt to celebrate the once unmentioned Mau Mau and to introduce into the political vocabulary of Kenya. Kenyatta was the Prime Minister, but "Mau Mau could not be incorporated fully into the postcolonial power knowledge consideration because their men who had inherited colonial power had been some of its staunch opponents."[16]

The novel was originally written in Gikuyu and later got translated by Goro. The very fact that the novel is dedicated to all those committed to the development of literature in languages of African people shows the novelist's interest in the recreation of African culture, ethos, language and heroism. The novelist wants to preserve African cultural values on one hand and make them understand his vision of socialist world. In other words, says Goodwin, "There is a latent theory in Ngugi that cultural expression is a bound by which can be an index of the quality of social and political life."[17]

Matigari is a modern figure also. He is a warrior who participated in the Mau Mau movement and won freedom for Kenya. Soon he comes to know about the corrupt world in the postcolonial Kenyan society. So he would wage a war against the present government that continues the colonial practice of using the army and police to hunt down the recalcitrant Mau Mau generals. The group of generals and writers who waged a war against the neo-colonial Kenyan government were known as the Matigari.

So in the new Kenyan society the Matigaris would observe the turn of events in Kenya and wait for an opportune time to return and restore the reign of justice and truth and so every year,

> With the goading of songs and popular discourse and even the magazines such as the last African edition of *Drum*, we awaited the inevitable return of the Matigari who could complete the project of the independence.[18]

The main thrust of the novel is on the right of the growers to enjoy the fruits but not the masters. When the workers come to know that they are being exploited, they do not hesitate to wage a war against the oppressors. It is to assert that those who sow have the right to enjoy the full use of their labour and to put an end to the oppression that prevents them from doing so. The enemy here is not a White settler alone but the African who represents western capitalism and its compressor packages. The novel ultimately repudiates any route to liberation that falls short of an armed uprising. The enemy can never be driven by words alone. No matter how sound the argument may be, the novelist takes an increasingly uncompromising stance with regard to the oppressed ones. Justice for the oppressed comes from a sharpened spear. This statement is echoed by Gikandi: "Justice for the oppressed springs up from the armed might of the united dispossessed. This is the protagonist quest's for truth and justice." (103) Matigari concerns himself with the oppression faced by the Gikuyu community. He earnestly feels that those who sow are alone eligible to enjoy the full use of the fruits of their labour. Unfortunately, the Kenyan independence has not brought any good to the workers and peasants.

However, their labour runs like nectar in a sieve. The neocolonial Kenyan men and women exploit them. Having fought against the colonial rule, Matigari returns to discover that injustice still exists all through in different forms in the realms of business, education, and religion. So he goes back to the forest and decides to fight back for justice to the fellow Africans. The primary exploiters are Muriuki wa Ngaruro, an absurd minister of Truth and Justice.

As Matigari observes most of the people in the Kenyan society, he comes across everyone failing him. During the meeting, the minister of Truth and Justice exemplifies the deeply authoritarian nature of the government. The minister goes to the extent of proposing a ban on sexual life of people. The workers face indignities and lead life of exploitation. Matigari himself observes the pitiable conditions of the Kenyan society.

> The country has a good international image in the west because of its rule of 'truth and justice.' The meeting had therefore drawn observers from the ruling political parties of the western countries. They sat in the front row seats so that they could properly see how the workers in the third world country could be silenced with instant truth and justice. *Mg*, 100

Here Matigari feels that there isn't any need on the part of Kenyan administrators to invite the western countries.

Even in the realm of religion, one notices the exploitative nature of the African Christianity which has been used to rationalise imperialist domination and exploitation of peasants and workers. The novelist makes use of the Biblical framework of the story and incorporates the author's message. It also dominates his use of the image. Matigari's miraculous religion proves to have been brought above by human agencies. The breaking of the bread is linked directly to a traditional use of communalism thus: "Great love I saw there among the women and children . . . when a bean fell we would share it among ourselves." (55-56) The Africans who were supposed to share food among themselves have become so selfish that they did not approve of sharing their food by the fellow Africans.

The agony of Matigari is such that he comments on the exploitative nature of both the Europeans and the Africans. He becomes critical of the testament of covenant the both entered with one another. After winning independence, Some Africans break the convenant by behaving like the Whites. Matigari, a middle-aged, tall and well-built leader who over a wide brimmed hat strapped under his Chui expresses his agony through his songs, sings thus: "Great love I saw there among the women and children . . . we shared even the single bean that fell upon the ground." (55-56)

He observed the people, who were lured, put to many traps under temptations. Thus Matigari represents a hero who waged a war against the Whites and won independence for Kenya. Soon he went round the society and observed the people being exploited by the neo-colonialists. So he expressed his deep-felt convictions.

Ngugi shows how the early black pro-Christians in an attempt to prove how good Christians they are, have tried to suppress mercilessly their own native customs than even the British have done. In *The River Between*, a group of people on the pretext of upholding the native traditions exploit the innocent public for their personal ends. In *Weep Not, Child*, Jacobo tries to suppress Ngotho cruelly and hinders the early attempts of the blacks to get back their occupied lands. The cruel ways of homeguards during the Mau Mau emergency to suppress the natives are portrayed vividly in *Weep Not, Child* and *A Grain of Wheat*. *Petals of Blood*, *Devil on the Cross* and *Matigari* deal with the African elite who have adopted the European ways of exploiting the Africans.

Ngugi's characters suffer, struggle and revolt against the exploitation both by the Whites and their fellow Africans in all his novels. Their revolt against the exploitation is dealt with in the sixth chapter.

NOTES

1. Arthur Ravenscroft, *Ngugi wa Thiong'o: Contemporary Novelist* (London: Saint James Press, 1991), p. 695.
2. C.B. Robson, *Ngugi wa Thiong'o* (London: Macmillan, 1979), p. 12.
3. Jomo Kenyatta, *Facing Mount Kenya* (London: Mercury, 1961), p. 99.
4. Corinthians, *The Holy Bible*, 15: 36.
5. Robson, p. 51.
6. D. Elders, "A Review of *A Grain of Wheat*," *ALT*, No. 1 (1968), p. 52.

7. W.J. Howard, "Themes and Development in the Novels of Ngugi," *Critical Evaluation of African Literature* (London: Heinemann, 1973), pp. 116-17.
8. David Cook, *Ngugi wa Thiong'o: An Exploration of his Writings* (London: Heinemann, 1983), p. 69.
9. G.D. Killam, *An Introduction to the Writings of Ngugi wa Thiong'o* (London: Heinemann. 1980), p. 96.
10. Ravenscroft, *Ngugi*, p. 695.
11. Robson, p. 104.
12. Eustace Palmer, *A Growth of African Novel* (London: Heinemann, 1979), p. 78.
13. Ngugi wa Thiong'o, *Detained: A Writer's Prison Dairy* (London: Heinemann, 1981), p. 8.
14. Odun Balogun, "Ngugi's *Devil on the Cross*, The Novel as Hagiography of Marxism" *UFAHAMU*, Vol. 16, No. 2 (1988), p. 87.
15. Simon Gikandi, "The Epistemology of Translation: Ngugi's *Matigari* and Politics of Language," *RAL*, Vol. 12, No. 1 (Spring 1991) pp. 161-62.
16. K.L. Goodwin, "Nationality-Chauvinism Must Burn! Utopian Visions in *Petals of Blood* and *Matigari*," *Literary Criterion* (1991) p. 11.
17. Gikandi, p. 102.

Chapter 5

Exploitation of the African Women

Since times immemorial, women have been the victim of male domination and oppression and have been treated as objects of pleasure. Man always looked down upon her as the weaker sex, servile to him. Different societies of the world have given a sanction to the subjugation of women at the hands of men. *The Holy Bible* says, "wives submit yourselves to your husbands as to the lord."[1] *The Holy Quran* makes a similar statement:

> Men are superior to women on account of the qualities with which God has gifted the one, above the other. . . . Virtuous women are obedient, careful during their husband's absence because God hath on them being careful.[2]

In some western societies, an organised fight for women's rights for equality with men was fought. In certain societies, the condition of women never changed. African women were perhaps the most exploited section of women in the world, exploited on the basis of race, class and gender. Ngugi's portrayal of exploited Kenyan women is powerful and varied. In spite of being attractive and independent, all his major women characters without any exception are sufferers and victims of exploitation either directly or indirectly in colonial and neo-colonial imperialistic Kenya. Kenyan women, in his novels, are exploited not only by the Europeans but also by their own race.

Exploitation of African women in the early stages of colonial period has been more on the basis of race than on the basis of gender and class. He starts with the portrayal of the effect of cultural exploitation by the Europeans on the African women. Racial exploitation in the form of cultural exploitation is brought about clearly in Ngugi's *The River Between*. The novel concerns itself with Kenya of nineteen twenties and thirties, when young girls were exposed to constant anti-circumcision propaganda and at the same time they were under pressure in their African communities to perform complete ritual of circumcision. The drastic effect of such conditions on the two young Kenyan girls—Nyambura and Muthoni—is described in the novel.

Nyambura and Muthoni, as daughters of Joshua, an early African convert into Christianity, were not allowed to undergo the tribal custom of circumcision. They were not even permitted to listen to the songs and dances connected to it. According to the Gikuyu custom, no proper Gikuyu can dream of marrying a girl who has not been circumcised. Muthoni wanted to get married as other girls of the tribe, according to the traditional custom. Going through circumcision ritual, she wanted to be a woman 'made beautiful in the tribe.' She did not like her father's suppression in this matter. So she questions her sister:

> Father and mother are circumcised. But why are they stopping me? Why do they deny me this? How could I be outside the tribe when all the girls born with me at the same time have left me. (44)

Muthoni rebelled against the oppressive authority of her father and said to her sister, Nyambura, who thought that circumcision was a sin:

> I too have embarrassed the White mans' faith. . . . You learn the way of the tribe. Yes . . . the White mans' God does not quite satisfy me. I want, I need something more. My life and your life are here, in the hills that you and I know. (26)

Deculturisation of the natives by the Europeans made her feel uprooted from the tradition. She experienced herself alienated from the tribe while following some other religion. She tried to identify herself with the traditional custom of circumcision along with the other girls living on ridges there.

In an attempt to reconcile 'many forces that wanted to control her,' Muthoni breaks away from paternal authority to get circumcised and runs away to her aunt's house. She refused to come back from there when she is given the last chance by her father. She talks about her plight:

> No, none will understand. I say I am a Christian and my father and mother have followed the new faith. I have not run away from that. But I also want to be initiated into the ways of the tribe. (43)

Muthoni's father, as a preacher of Christian principles, wants people there to understand how Christian he is, and is not able to understand the agony of his daughter. Even when her wound gets infected and her health deteriorates, she doesn't get fatherly affection from Joshua. Unhappy Miriam and Nyambura have to make visits to Muthoni without Joshua's knowledge. Unfortunately, Muthoni's wound doesn't heal and she falls into delirium, unable to make her family understand her religious attitude. She tells her sister: "Tell Nyambura, I see Jesus. And I am a woman made beautiful in the tribe." (53)

The act of circumcision, a commonplace event in the tribe, is of crucial importance to Muthoni as an individual. Through this event, she experiences a revelation: she has seen Jesus. In the process to integrate the conflicting faith of Christianity and the way of the tribe, she pays a heavy price of death. Muthoni's death causes a sense of despair and gloom in the family. It brings a void in the heart of Nyambura.

Nyambura gets vexed with Joshua's religion which has neither love nor humanity. She too, like Muthoni, breaks away from paternal authority, proclaiming love openly for Waiyaki, who has true love and genuine concern for her and for the people of ridges. But the very fact that she is not circumcised makes the union of Waiyaki and Nyambura in the form of marriage, unacceptable to 'Kiama,' a secret society that has aroused after the death of Muthoni, to get rid of the influence of White man on the ways of ridges. Kabonyi, the leader of 'Kiama' brings Nyambura and Waiyaki before the public on the charge that circumcised Waiyaki, being the member of Kiama, has violated the oath by offering to marry uncircumcised Nyambura and thus has committed a great sin. Unable to win beautiful Nyambura himself, Kamau, son of Kabonyi tries to quench his thirst for revenge against Nyambura's lover, in the name of Kiama's principles. Death is the punishment for those who violated the sacred promise of Kiama. To Waiyaki, Nyambura looked like a lamb on an altar of sacrifice. Nyambura thus becomes a victim to religious clashes between the Christian missionaries and the traditional Kenyans.

Nyambura's father did not make any attempt to save his daughter. Thus both Nyambura and Muthoni became victims of cultural exploitation. As a submissive wife of pro-Christian Joshua, Miriam has to suffer witnessing disintegration of her family and loss of her two daughters.

The Europeans also infused colour complex into the minds of African women. They equated African black colour with that of devils. The impact of colour consciousness induced by the colonists into the minds of African women is devastatingly described in Ngugi's *Devil on the Cross*. Wariinga, the protagonist in the *Devil on the Cross*, indulges in self-pity that her appearance is the root-cause of all her misfortunes and troubles.

> What she hated most was her blackness, so she would disfigure her body with skin-lighting creams like 'Umbi' and 'Snow fire' . . . now her body was covered with light and dark spots like the guinea fowl. Her hair was splitting and it has borrowed the colour of moleskin because it has been straightened with red-hot iron combs. (11)

Besides, spoiling her skin and hair, she tries to hide her teeth with her lips tightly and cannot laugh freely because of the inferiority complex, she develops. She is not able to recognise her own beauty in all its naturalness.

> But when Wariinga was happy and forgot to worry about the fading whiteness of her teeth and about the blackness of her skin and laughed with all her heart, her laughter completely disarmed the people. (11)

These lines throw light on Wariinga's physique, which is naturally attractive. Wariinga, unable to appreciate sheer splendour of her beauty, indulged in crushing self-pity and self-doubt about her appearance. As a result, she lost confidence and felt alienated. She could not respect her own body and herself and ultimately attempted suicide.

Ngugi portrays the sufferings of African women during the most oppressive and exploitative conditions during emergency in *Weep Not, Child* and *A Grain of Wheat*. During 'the suppressive times,' Mwihaki's father, Jacobo indulges in punishing the Africans taking side of the White government. Young Mwihaki is not able to spend time with her father in those days. The distance grows between the two as the days pass by. She hears the African begging her father for mercy in terror. Those are the cries of death. Even Jacobo fears death at the hands of the fellow Africans. The cries of fear of death surround her from all sides. At that time, she says to Njoroge:

> I am caught in it and if this goes on, I feel as if I could go mad. . . . I am telling this to show you how glad I am at the prospects of escaping from it all. (127)

Mwihaki's case is similar to that of a young French woman described by Frantz Fanon in the colonial war and mental disorder in his book, *The Wretched of the Earth*. The French girl says:

> My father was highly in civil service . . . sometimes . . . he would eat nothing at all and not even sleep. He was in such a state of excitement over putting down the rebellion. . . . Algerians were being tortured. . . . I used to wonder, how it was that a human being was able to bear hearing those screams of pain . . . quite apart from the actual torture and so it went on. Finally, I did not even go home. I know almost all the families that lived there. In the end, I didn't dare to walk in the street any more. I was sure meeting hatred anywhere.[3]

Like this girl, Miwihaki says to Njoroge, son of Ngotho, that everybody tries to avoid her. She begins to feel the guilt of her father's action against his own race living around them. When Njoroge's father becomes an enemy to Jacobo, her friendship with fellow Africans is affected. Mwihaki also suffers the death of her father in the most tactful political entanglements created by Howlands between Ngotho's son and Jacobo to destroy them both.

During the emergency, not only young girls like Mwihaki, but also elderly women suffered. During the curfew, Nganga in *Weep Not, Child*, was taken away from the bed by White soldiers. Wives of Nganga went from one homeguard post to the next asking them to be allowed to see their husband. They suffered in fear and in long waiting for their husband, only to hear the death of their husband with five other men in the forest.

Women were imprisoned to make their men suffer. Though it is not a big crime to go out at six O'clock in the evening during the emergency, Njeri and her son Koro were imprisoned when they just came out of the house to search Boro. When the fine imposed was paid, Njeri alone was released. This is all to hurt Ngotho's feelings as a husband of Njeri and father of Koro. Again when Jacobo was murdered, both Njere and Nyokobi, wives of Ngotho, were arrested.

During the emergency time, Africans were reduced economically by the Whites. Njeri and Nyokobi could not understand why the Whites reduced them economically and why they imprisoned their innocent young children who had not committed any crime.

> 'Why do they oppress the Black people?' Njeri bitterly asked. She was growing old. Her days of poverty and hardship are being made heavier by this anxiety. (79)

Njeri and Nyokobi's husband had been thoroughly beaten up by the Whites to extract information about the murder of Jacobo. The wives watched their husbands who suffered both physically and mentally, unable to resist the colonial suppression. They finally suffered the death of Ngotho as his wives. Juliana in *Weep Not, Child* also suffered the death of her husband in the exploitative political conditions by the White colonist Howlands who used Jacobo as a pan in the game to suppress his fellow Africans like Ngotho.

All the hopes that Njeri and Nyokobi pinned on Nojoroge that he would get himself well educated and would lift up their family's economic position and status shuddered. They had finally to save their disillusioned son from committing suicide.

They were not able to fulfil their desires and watched the disintegration of the family under the oppressive inhuman attitude of the White colonists.

Even in *A Grain of Wheat*, the colonists put women to task. The image of an old mother suffering the death of her only young and strong son Githogo is portrayed in Chapter I of the novel. White soldiers who surrounded Thabi and Rungai killed him, when he ran to save his helpless mother from the cruelty of the European and African soldiers.

Mumbi's happy married life with hard-working and sincere Gikonyo, whom she chose among her many worthy suitors, came to an end with his arrest by White soldiers.

> She found herself powerless to save her man. She collected all her will and strength into a cry . . . the cry was like a shriek of terror. And this feverish terror seized the whole of Thabai as later in the night they learned that Gitogo, the deaf-and-dumb son of the old woman had been shot dead by those messengers of whiteman's peace. (103-4)

Mumbi lived under constant fear even when her husband was with her at the possibility of her husband being taken away by the White soldiers any time. Now, the possibility of Gikonyo's death at the hands of White soldiers like the death of other detainees made her suffer more. Added to this, the people of Thabi were subjugated to horrible ripples of terror by the White soldiers and the black homeguards. The indirect suffering of the black women in the village is no less than what their men suffered directly at the hands of oppressing White soldiers.

After the men in Thabi village were arrested, their women were not left with even a piece of land from which they could earn their living. Heavy taxes were also imposed on them. Children stopped their education, unable to meet the expenditure on it. In such conditions, women struggled to feed the aged and children at home. A woman in *A Grain of Wheat* cries in vain to meet the M.P. in the town, every day spending all her time there with hungry stomach.

While mothers suffered thus, young women like Wambuku suffered waiting for their men when they were held up as Mau Mau warriors in the forest or when they were shot dead. Mumbi recalls the whole thing before Mugo:

> Kihika was arrested and hanged on a tree, something strange came over her. For a few days she never left her home, and when she did so, eventually, well, she only destroyed herself with soldiers and homeguards. But she refused, so it is said, the advances of this particular homeguard, who got his chance for revenge during the trench. She never recovered from that beating and died three months later in pregnancy. (137)

Wambuku thought patriotic Kihika had betrayed colourful rainbow of her hopes and desires, unable to keep his promise that he would live forever with her. The exploitative and suppressive conditions caused psychological damage to her. She became a victim of sexual exploitation by homeguards. Women like Njeri sacrificed their lives in cause of their wearied lovers. Njeri ran away to the forest to fight at Kihika's side. Soon after Kihika's death, she too was dead.

Not only Wambuku, all the people of Thabi village were hit by the violence of homeguards and White government in one way or the other. In the words of Govind Narayan Sharma: "A considerable portion of Ngugi's novel is devoted to the portrayal of violence that was done not merely to the body—the lands, home and hearts of the Gikuyu people—but also their soul in the form of a spiritual suffering and agony inflicted on them by the White man."[4]

The condition of Kenya during the Emergency is described by Kigonda, a farm labourer in Ngugi's powerful play, *I Will Marry When I Want*. We see this atmosphere of emergency in *A Grain of Wheat*.

> That the state of emergency was declared over Kenya
> Our patriots,
> Men and women of
> Limuru and the whole country
> Were arrested
> The emergency laws became very oppressive

Our homes were burnt down
We were jailed
We were taken to detention camps
Some of us were crippled through beating
Other were castrated
Our women were raped
Our wives and daughters were raped before our eyes. (27)

Women and children of Thabi village in *A Grain of Wheat* were arrested by White district officer Robson to vacate their huts and move into a new place within the given time. Their huts were burnt down when they were sleeping at night. Mumbi describes the sadism of homeguards when they splashed petrol on her hut, which was already dry.

> The leader of the homeguards struck a match and threw it at the roof. It did not light, and the others laughed at him. They shouted and encouraged him. One of them tried to take matches from him to demonstrate how it could be done. It became a game between them. At the fourth or fifth attempt the roof caught fire. (140)

When the fire spread to other huts, women were not able to scream. At odd hours they were left to sit and groan without a place to hide themselves from the evil eyes of White soldiers and homeguards. The burning away of the huts has been more than the loss of money and security to Mumbi's mother-in-law.

> For those huts meant much to her because she had built them after Waruhius, her husband in the Rift Valley, had divorced her from his side. (140)

Burning the house means removing old thoughts from their minds which they have shared with their men. When they moved to a new place, it would be difficult for their men to search for them after they come back from detention camps. Thus Thabi village was completely demolished. The punishment to Thabi village was a warning to other villages, never to give food or any kind of help to those black men fighting against the White government. Mumbi said:

> We were prisoners in the village, and the soldiers had built their camps all round to prevent any escape. We went without food. The cry of children was terrible to hear. (143-44)

Even children were not spared from whipping. All were made to dig trenches within the given time. To escape from this communal labour, women mostly tried to work in European farmhouses, tea-plantations and digging Muthangari grass for White people. Thus Thabi women were forced to become workers in various fields.

In the highly disturbed Thabi village, Mumbi describes the constant fear and threat she has faced along with other women there.

> The new D.O. did not mind the cries. He even permitted soldiers to pick women and carry them to their tents. God! I didn't know how I escaped from that ignominy. Every night I prayed that such a thing should never happen to me. Wambuku died in the trench. They took her body and threw it into a grave dug a few yards from the trench. (144)

Forced labour led to sexual harassment. Cruel White soldiers, African homeguards and even their officer Thomson Robson picked up women as articles in the market area. The African women's opposition to such kind of harassment is put to an end by beating them till they die as in Wambuku's case. Then hunger deaths occurred, a number of women "secretly and voluntarily offered themselves to the soldiers for a little food." (146)

Thus not only the Whites, even the Africans exploited the helpless African women ruthlessly. The forceful exploitation of African women by both the Whites and the Africans has been more during the Mau Mau Emergency, just before 'Uhuru.' E. Palmer rightly observes, the African society was cleverly thrown back into prostitution by the schemes of the White and the new black imperialists.[5]

In *The River Between*, there is no indication of sexual exploitation of black women except once when Muthoni points out to Livingstone, head of the missionary there, that the circumcised women of the church are his many wives. The inaccessible land of hills and ridges in *Weep Not, Child* is opened up by long broad tarmac road linking up Gikuyu land to the lands beyond. This road has laid the path for sexual exploitation of African women by Asians also in addition to the Europeans and African homeguards. Even when the road was under construction in *Weep Not, Child*, the Italian prisoners who built the road indulged in sexual exploitation and left a name for themselves by leaving White children to African women they slept with. This mixed breed was looked down upon during those days. It was said:

> Only the children by black mothers and Italian prisoners who were also white men were not really 'white' in the usual way. They were ugly and some grew up to have small wounds . . . this was a punishment. Black women should not sleep with white men who ruled them and treated them badly. (6)

The White settler Holland in *Weep Not, Child*, during his wife's absence, picked up African women and exploited them sexually. In *A Grain of Wheat*, African women are sexually exploited by their own race.

Karanja, the leader of homeguards, tried to exploit Mumbi sexually. He mocked often at Mumbi's hope of Gikonyo's coming back from detention. Mumbi checked his arrogant advances with great difficulty. Once he called her and said that her husband would come back soon. The grateful Mumbi was overwhelmed with joy and was prepared to do anything. Karanja seduced her and when she realised what had happened, it was already late. Mumbi's situation is similar to that of the protagonist in Ngugi's powerful short story, "The Return," where the woman believes that her husband was dead and so she agrees to marry her husband's friend when he proposes to her. Certainly, Mumbi is placed above her. But Mumbi's husband, on his return from the detention camp, could not understand her properly. Jabbi comments:

> For her single affair with Karanga was no adultery after all since he has exploited his position as a chief and her dazed anxiety over her husband's too suddenly eminent return from so many of years

> of detention. These revelations thus complicate the moral perspectives bearing upon the Gikonyo-Mumbi plot in which Gikonyo's own breeding sleeve of jealousy has been the only known factor setting the tone so far in the narrative. Mumbi's story is thus reminiscence, a flashback that also induces a valuable sense, a moral scrutility or complexity in the novel.[6]

The exploitative colonial conditions changed the whole pattern of her lovely married life with Gikonyo. Mumbi, carrying the name after the Gikuyu mother, did not abandon the innocent child. Her son, through Karanja, became the barrier to their marital relationship. Her husband grew bitter towards her. But she does everything to keep her husband in good humour. Unfortunately, her husband remains indifferent to her and calls her a whore in a desperate mood. A critic rightly observes,

> The life of Gikonyo and Mumbi is one of the most significant points of attention in *A Grain of Wheat* because it enlarges the traditional conflict between man and woman in society and prescribes solution, which is still relevant to the entire situation in the novel. The most important prescription is recognition of equality and mutual cooperation.[7]

Mumbi, here, is like Ibsen's Nora in *A Doll's House*, who having got disillusioned in marriage with her husband, goes out breaking herself as an individual responsible for herself first and then to the world. Ngugi is advocating here, equality between the sexes and mutual understanding and cooperation of both the man and wife in married life.

Ngugi thus sketches Mumbi as a most beautiful woman of the ridges and makes her a victim as a wife waiting in distressed conditions for her husband who was detained without trial for a long time. She also suffers as a victim of sexual exploitation during the emergency in Kenya and even after his return in the marital relationship. This sexual exploitation portrayed in *A Grain of Wheat* takes a different turn in the next novel, *Petals of Blood*. Wanja in this novel is not a straight girl. She is a barmaid and a prostitute whose salary is regulated, but is paid according to the whims of the employer. She is a ruthlessly exploited Kenyan woman.

With the portrayal of Wanja in *Petals of Blood*, Ngugi starts his depiction of the most exploitative section of the African women in African society under neo-colonial or imperialistic conditions. Generally, prostitutes are condemned as a race of sinful, infectious females by society. People look down upon them. Ngugi wants people to examine the causes behind prostitution, rising above the superficial understanding of the problem. Besides this, he wants prostitutes to realise the causes of their degeneracy and wants them to fight against them. He is on the side of the most oppressed. He says:

> Generally, in fiction, one tries to portray those people who seem to be exceptions of the norm . . . what I tried to do in my novels is to show the dielectic relationship between various aspects of society and reality. When I take a prostitute, I want to show that she is a product of all forces impinging on that society.[8]

The concept of prostitution is new to polygamous African society. The exploitation of the African women, sexually, during the colonial time by the White settlers, White soldiers and even by the missionary people, slowly led to the rise of prostitution. In the postcolonial times, the rise of bourgeoisie class among the Africans, rise of bars and tourism, fostered the profession of prostitution in imperialistic Kenya.

Colonisation deprived the African woman of her traditional status. Even the capitalist economy changed her role as a producer of goods. In the pre-colonial Kenya where private property and class structure were not developed, women used to have considerable economic independence and freedom over the products they produced along with men. Killam writes: "The growing division of labour in the modern economic sector is widening the gap in productivity and in income between them. The status of women is therefore lower in relation to that of men."[9] The secondary status given by the White colonisers and perpetuated by the African men even after attaining freedom, the increase in urbanisation, the craze for artificial life induced by the colonists changed the whole way of African women's living in imperialistic Kenya. Ngara comments: "Through Wanja, we are made to realise that capitalism is responsible for the rise of prostitution." (38)

Wanja is one of the many young girls who have fallen prey to the artificial ways of living. She easily becomes a prey to the amorous advances made by a wealthy friend of her father. Her mathematics teacher also exploits her situation and blackmails her by saying that he would report to her parents about her movements with the rich man if she does not agree to his advances. Soon, she becomes pregnant because of her fifth boy friend, who would make her his second wife but not his first wife. She, in utter despair, has to end her studies.

> In Kenya there is no programme in the school system or even in the community which provides the needs of teenage mothers. Immediately, after a girl is found to be pregnant, she is sent home.[10]

Unable to face her parents in guilt, she runs away from her house to her cousin who trades in flesh.

After independence, bars have sprung up everywhere in Kenya. However, the ill-treatment meted out to the barmaids remained the same. Wanja explains to Karaga, the misery in the lives of barmaids and the high exploitative nature of bar owners,

> There is only one song, sung by all barmaids—woe. They give you seventy-five shillings a month. They expect you to work for twenty-four hours. In the daytime you give beer and smiles to customers. In the evening you are supposed to give them yourself and sighs in bed. Bar and Lodging. The owner grabs twenty shillings for letting a couple use a Wano bed and torn sheets for ten minutes. (75-76)

Wanja becomes aware of the fact that in the long run, it is the men who triumphed and walked over her body with money. She therefore runs away from bars, having got vexed with them.

> In some respects Ngugi's character Wanja in *Petals of Blood* is the East African counterpart of Jugna Nana. Both women are strong personalities and both have considerable powers of seduction. The difference is that whereas for Jugna, the captivation of men is a principal source of personal satisfaction. Wanja has inhibitions.

> She is torn between living convincingly in the country and the greater opportunities of urban including sexual self-expression.[11]

In Illmorog, she lives among the innocent villagers. She seeks to conceive a child in vain. The prophecy of a sage that she can conceive a child on a full moon day in the fields fails. Her sense of alienation increases. Moreover, she who was formerly used to the city comfortable life is now disillusioned with the life in countryside. She wanted to go to the city, earn enough money to live, and come back to Illmorog to live comfortably there forever. But in the city, a German traps her cleverly. The novelist discusses the ill effects of tourism, particularly, the flesh trade.

Her father cared only for money. When Wanja wants to come back and lead a normal life, her father does not support her. Wanja gets disgusted with her father, who never shows the true concern of a father. Having no one to rely upon, she goes to the city to become a barmaid once again unwillingly. When her room is set on fire by unknown people, she comes back to Illmorog and starts brewing Thengeta drink along with Abdulla. When she makes a drink popular, Chui cancels license to her. Having been thus exploited by neo-colonial power, she is once again pushed to search a way to make her living.

Wanja believes firmly in the philosophy, 'you eat somebody or you are eaten.' So she opens up her own trade house, 'The Sunshine Lodge.' She joins hand with imperialists like Chui, Kimeria and Mizo to worship God Mammon.

> It is origin of Sunshine Lodge, that elegant brothel between Cape Town and New Jerusalem . . . eat or to be eaten Wanja becomes wealthy and powerful. Not only hypocrisy is dramatised but the progressive deterioration of the moral horizon in direct proportion to the consideration of development of new Illmorog.[12]

Her cynicism sinks deeper when she receives her early exploiters Kimeria and Chui along with other customers. She is quite adept in the craft, particularly in attracting men. When she tells Munira and Karega that she now operates as a prostitute with her philosophy, 'you sit on someone or somebody else will sit on you,' she echoes the ideas of Selina in Rebeka Njau's *Ripples in Pool.*

> Although I am free with them. They cannot cheat me. . . . They suck your blood, if you are a fool, leave you dry, always demanding in fact more than one can give. But they cannot treat me like that.[13]

Unlike Karaga who believes in a New Earth, Wanja wants to go with the tide without thinking of changing it into a new one.

Wanja in imperialistic Kenya, learnt to believe the philosophy 'you eat or you are eaten' and as a result, she travelled in the wrong direction and became thoroughly exploited and an alienated character. When she did a worthwhile thing to Illmorog people and found some meaning in her life, she realised her mistake of blaming others for what has happened to her. At the end of the novel, she changes her philosophy for good. But Jacica Wariinga, whose life pattern in certain ways coincides with that of Wanja, takes a positive route early in her life, realising the things to become a fully developed self-respected individual in *Devil on the Cross*.

Ngugi did not portray much about African women suffering in polygamous society. But in *A Grain of Wheat*, the cruel treatment of an economically poor man in polygamous society towards his unwanted wife is portrayed in a brief yet powerful way. Wangari, Gikonyo's mother, lived in Elbourgean area with her husband who worked on European farms.

> He gets new brides and complained that the thighs of the first wife did not yield warmth any more. He beat her, hoping that this would drive her away. Wangari stuck on. Eventually Waruhia ordered her to leave his home and crushed mother and son to a life of ever-wandering on God's earth. (158)

Miriam in *Petals of Blood* unable to tolerate the exploitative nature of her husband breaks away from him. She speaks of the burden under which she lived.

> She complains about her triple duties to her child, Ndinguri, to her husband and to her European landlord . . . expected to work on the European farm; to work on her own piece of land: and to keep the home in unity, health and piece. (11)

It was the pressure under which most of the women characters in Illmorog lived in *Petals of Blood*. Later she did not allow herself to be exploited by brother Ezekiel.

Wariinga in *Devil on the Cross* was vibrated and beautiful like Wanja. Like Wanja, she too is sexually exploited while she was still young and innocent at school. Through the story of Mahua Kareendi, Wariinga describes that she has been exploited sexually by men in imperialistic Kenya. When she was young, a young boy at school exploited her. A rich old man, who used to come to their house, encouraged by her own uncle, exploits Wariinga sexually. When she approached this old man who used to play the hunter and the hunted game with her, he said:

> How could you possibly have conceived as soon if I were the only man who went with you. . . . I thought all along that I was going with a clean school girl, a girl I would have loved to marry so that she could be balm for my old bones. But instead, I picked on Kareendi. Ready-to-yield, did I? (146)

Unlike Wanja who threw her child in latrine pit, Wariinga did not abandon the child. She had understanding parents to support her. She learnt typewriting and went in search of a job from one place to another. But everywhere, she faced a similar situation. She was asked to join a modern love bar and lodging that has become the main employment bureau for girls like her. She rejected them all. At last, she joined as a typist. Her boss Kihira was a church person. He too proposed to her to be his 'sugar girl' tempting her by offering luxuries. He tried to exploit her economically poor condition. When she refused and resisted his luring attempts, she was thrown out of job.

In utter despair, she went to her lover in university. He earlier agreed with her child and expressed words of true love. All her hope to carve her life beautifully is shattered when he rejects her thus:

> A chameleon will always be a chameleon. A girl who starts going with men old enough to be her father while she is at school to the extent of giving birth to babies when still a student . . . no you are

> spinning me this yarn only because Waigoko has refused to let you continue making his bed in hostels for modern love. (25)

Betrayed thus, she resolves never to have affairs with any man. On the same day, the owner of the house hired three thugs who threw her and her goods out, as she refused to increase the rent of the house immediately. She said she would pay only after a reference to the rent tribunal for settlement.

Unable to live in the debased city, Wariinga went back to her native place in Illmorog. She saw a devil in her dream. The devil in the dream represents symbolically all the evils in the world in the form of monopoly capitalism. While travelling by Mwara's 'Matatu' (taxi) along with Wangari, Muthuri and Gathuiria, they decide to go to Illmorog cave where a competition among the imperialists is conducted under the name 'Devil's Feast.'

Ngugi depicts the exploitation of the African women at the hands of other Africans. In the cave, he describes the barmaids who are made to appear as dolls with skin-tight dresses before the thieves. In the world where love and sex have becomc the things that can be purchased easily, the word 'love' has lost importance. Barmaids wore bands inscribed 'I love you' in an exploitative sense.

In the 'Devil's Cave' it is revealed how the thieves indulge in exploitation of women. The thieves there have to reveal number of wives and mistresses they have and also the cases of adultery and sin they have indulged in. Ndaaya wa Kahuria is well trained in snatching the purses of women in public places. Gitutu wa Gataanguru says that his old arrogant father would send for any beautiful woman he sees to make her his mistress. As far as himself having mistresses, he argues like Satan who quotes from the *Bible* to win his argument with Eve. He says: "he, who keeps something in reserve, never goes hungry and when a European gets old, he likes to eat veal." (99)

The institution of marriage has lost its significance among the exploitative thieves. There are also certain women from bourgeoisie class who have become "Ready to Yield" kind. Those women do not have much work to do. In their hunt for five minutes' love or an hour's love, they have degraded in their moral values and had joined exploitative section of people. They robbed another section of women of their husbands. Those men spend time with these 'good time' girls and did not care for their wives. Thus degeneration of some women belonging to bourgeoisie class is also drawn focussed on.

Nyakinua, Wanja's grandmother in *Petals of Blood*, lived on her piece of ancestral lands. In the development scheme of Illmorog, her lands were grabbed. In an attempt to get them back, she dies. Thus she becomes a victim of neo-colonial economic programs in Kenya. In *Devil on the Cross* also, Wangari's lands were confiscated. She was unable to pay back a loan of five thousand shillings to the Kenyan Economic Progress Bank. The rate of interest was very high. So her two acres of land was confiscated. She went in search of a job to Nairobi. When she approached an African, she said:

> the only job he could offer me was that of spreading my legs, that women with mature bodies were experts at that job. I felt a tear drop to the ground. (42)

Later another black man handed her over to the police. This patriotic woman who had never stolen anything was asked to pay fine by European judge on the charge that she was roaming in Nairobi without an identity card. Thus she too becomes a victim like Nyakinyua in *Petals of Blood* of the neo-colonial exploitative economic banks.

Ngugi portrays Guthera in *Matigari* who was sexually exploited like Wanja in *Petals of Blood* and Wariinga in *Devil on the Cross*. Unlike Wanja who was from the beginning arrogant, Guthera was a girl of church with high morals before she allows herself to be sexually exploited as a barmaid.

Her 'Father on Earth' was taken by police on the charge that he was a terrorist. When Guthera went to see him in the prison, the police t tried to exploit her distressed, helpless condition.

> Give me your purity, and I will give your parent back to you. The young maiden remained silent. The superintendent explained further: you are carrying your father's life between your legs. (35)

When she refused to be exploited thus, her 'Father on Earth' was put to death. Unable to feed the other children of her 'Father on Earth,' she begged the church people for help. She was not able to feed and clothe them properly. Several days, they went without food. It was only when she decided to 'walk on street,' she was able to feed the children.

The novelist throws light on the police who symbolise brutality and oppression. Two cops who were after defenceless Guthera lead their dogs on her mercilessly. Even the people in the street observed

> the police leashing terror on her. She was kneeling on the ground. The dog would leap towards her . . . some people laughed seeming to find the spectacle highly entertaining. A gush of urine rushed down her legs; she was staring death in the face. (30)

The police, who are expected to protect a lone woman like Guthera in such a condition, unleashed such a terror on her in the broad daylight in the main thoroughfare of the city in full public view. This speaks volumes about the nature of the people and the exploitative nature of policemen in independent Kenya. Gutheria swears thus:

> I will never go to bed with a policeman. I will take money from strangers, thieves, murderers even, but I will never open my legs for any policeman, these traitors no matter how much they are prepared to pay for the favours. This will be my eleventh commandment. (37)

Gutheria expresses her gratitude to Matigari, who helped her in the time of need. She broke her eleventh commandment in order to help Matigari and others to escape from the prison. She has given herself as a sacrificial lamp for his salvation. She realises how mean her life has been without definite purpose. She says:

> I have not been satisfied with the kind of life I have been leading. You see, my entire life has been dominated by men, be they our Father in Heaven, my Father on Earth, the priest or all the men who have bought my body and turned me into their mistress. (140)

When self-realisation came to Gathera, she was able to recognise the common pressures under which women in general lived. Rightly does she observe:

> The most important thing is not just to know that my life has been without meaning. I would say that there is not a woman who doesn't really know the pressures that we women live under. (140)

Here too, she has been a mattress on which the men who bought her rubbed their feet. Her troubles and social conditions have forced her to lead such a life. She wore 'blinkers like a horse' and lived life like an animal. Now she has recognised the new power in her as a woman.

Guthera, in a way, becomes the mouthpiece of the novelist. In fact, Ngugi wants women to recognise themselves as human beings first and then change their lives as second sex to become equal with men. Guthera sacrifices her life along with Matigari in an attempt to drive away the imperialists in Kenya rising thus to the position of a patriot. Guthera dies leaving the question to the women everywhere.

> I want to do something to change whatever it is that makes people live like animals, especially us women. What can we as women do to change our lives? Or will we continue to follow the paths carved out for us by men? Aren't we, the majority, any way? (140)

These lines exhibit the feminist assertions of Guthera to preserve the rights of women.

Ngugi did not idealise family lives of White settlers like Howlands or Thompson nor the family lives of the imperialists. Just as Thompson's wife in *A Grain of Wheat* had an extra-marital affair, in *Matigari*, the wife of Minister of Truth and Justice had an affair with her car driver. In her general address to the women, she urged "all women to take refuge in the safety of the church and to stop competing with their husband in drinking and adultery. Women were the cornerstones of the home." (27) But she herself was caught committing adultery with her driver in the back seat of the car outside the city. Guthera speaks of man's double standards and generalises the condition of women:

> What problems we women have to go through wherever we are! When that woman goes home, her husband will beat her, demanding to know what she was doing in the wilderness with a man. (151)

Ngugi reveals how the African women have been exploited in the colonial and the neo-colonial Kenya on the basis of race, class and gender. His women characters become victims of exploitation, directly or indirectly. In *Weep Not, Child* and *The River Between*, women are victims of racial exploitation. In *A Grain of Wheat*, the women are exploited sexually both by the White colonists and the African homeguards. In *Petals of Blood*, Wanja, who is sexually exploited, takes cudgels against the exploitative city. In the *Devil on the Cross*, Wariinga, a victim of sexual exploitation, becomes vociferous against the society. In *Matigari*, Guthera is forced to trade with her flesh. The novelist thus identifies the problems of women by depicting "the forces of denigration and self-degeneration."[14]

NOTES

1. "Ephesians," *The Holy Bible*, 5:12.
2. G.M. Rodwell, *Quoran*, trans. (London: Everyman's Library, 1909), p. 145.
3. Frantz Fanon, *The Wretched of the Earth* (Harmondsworth: Penguin, 1967), p. 222.
4. Govind Narayan Sharma, "Ngugi's Christian Vision: Theme and Pattern in *A Grain of Wheat*," *African Literature Today*, No. 10 (1979), p. 168.
5. Eustace Palmer, "Ngugi's *Petals of Blood*," *African Literature Today*, No.10 (1979), p. 161.
6. Bu Buakei Jabbi, "Conrad's Influence on Betrayal in *A Grain of Wheat*," *Research in African Literature*, Vol. 2, No. 1 (Spring 1980), pp. 63-64.
7. Emmanuel Ngara, "The Portrayal of Women in African Literature," *UFAHAMU*, Vol. 10, 3, 1980, p. 38.
8. G. Martin, "Ngugi: Interview," *Kunapipi*, Vol. 3, No. 2 (1981), p. 156.

9. U.R. Onunwa, "The struggle for the liberation of women in third world nations: The ambiguity of the role of church," *UFAHAMU*, Vol. 10, No. 2 (1989), p. 49.
10. Margerete Ngau, "'Women's Participation in Education and National Development,' The Dilemma of Institutional Bias in Kenya," *UFAHAMU*, Vol. 16, No. 2 (1988), p. 12.
11. Kenneth Littie, *The Sociology of Urban Women's Image in African Literature* (London: Macmillan, 1980), p. 82.
12. Felix Muthali, "Continuity and Change in Conrad and Ngugi," *Kunapipi*, Vol. 3, No. 1 (1981), p. 103.
13. Rebeka Njau's, *Ripples in Pool* (London: Heinemann, 1972), pp. 1-2.
14. David Cook and Michael Okenimkpe, *Ngugi wa Thiong'o: An Exploration of His Writings* (London: Heinemann, 1983), p. 232.

Chapter 6

Revolt against Exploitation

In his eternal quest for freedom—in the physical and metaphysical terms—man sometimes resists and overcomes, sometimes succumbs to the conditions he is in. In the search for liberation, crossing confining mental boundaries is a prerequisite for the recovery of the lost selves. Colonialism as one such confining condition implies not just laws of political freedom. Its tentacles of power and control penetrate the labyrinths of the mind and consciousness. Colonising is thus an invasion of the mind as well.

The issue of colonialism is relevant in the present times for understanding the intersection of the culture, knowledge and power, the politics of colonialism and the hegemony of Europe in the colonial and the postcolonial context. While political independence implies the break-down of the visible imperial structure, engaging with the colonial experience in a postcolonial state of mind is an attempt at dismantling the invisible imperial structures of control.

In Africa, the imperial tradition is maintained by the international bourgeoisie using the multinational and the flag-waving native ruling classes. The economic and political dependence of the African neo-colonial bourgeoisie is reflected in its culture of apemanship and parrotry enforced on a restive population through police boots, barbed wire, a gowned clergy and judiciary. Their ideas have also spread to a corpus of state intellectuals and the academics of the neo-colonial establishment. The resistance tradition is being carried out by the peasantry and the proletariat aided by patriotic students and other progressive elements of the petty middle class. This resistance is reflected in their patriotic defence of the peasant roots of national culture, and in their defence of the democratic struggle in Kenya. In the works of Ngugi, the resistance tradition pervades and arouses the feelings of Africans.

In *The River Between*, Ngugi discusses the struggle waged by the Kenyans against the White settlers in the early times. He gives a graphic account of the ridges which symbolise 'great fertility and promise.' The land "is beautiful and young and fertile and has been unaffected by turbulent forces outside it." (*RB*, 20)

The people maintained their magic rituals and customs, but with the coming of 'the butterflies,' the Gikuyu culture and land undergo many changes. For Gikuyus, the land is very important. It is not just because of his economic possibilities, it is also akin to spiritual. As long as their land is undisturbed, there is harmony and unity in the land. But the advent of the White man spreads ripples of hysteria in the Gikuyu society.

> In the past years, things were changing. The patterns of seasons were broken . . . perhaps, it had to do with the White man and the blasphemous men of Mykuyu. (68)

Siriana becomes a centre of conversion. Already the White settlers have taken over the land around it. Some of the Gikuyus noticed the insidious process of the White settlers. They start grumbling at the White domination. They formed an organisation called 'Kiama' to curb the domination of the Whites. The members took an oath to guarantee their allegiance to the ways of the ridges and towards ridding the country of the influence of the White man. Kabonyi, who led the movement, decides to fight the Whites to get back their lands, and also to win power for the clan.

Kabonyi as a member of governing committee of schools, does not approve of the education system propounded by the White settlers and followed by Waiyaki. He asks a rhetorical question thus: "Do you think the education of the tribe and the wisdom you have received is in any way below that of the White man" (95). As a typical adherent to the Kenyan heritage and practices, Kabonyi sees that the Marioshoni (people's school) started by Waiyaki doesn't preserve the learning wisdom of the old, instead it would widen the gap that already existed in the tribe. He throws light on the fact that the White man's education is not at all necessary. He inspires his people thus:

> It was better to drive the White man from the hills altogether. Were the people afraid? Were there no warriors left in the tribe? He would lead them. That was why he formed the Kiama. He would rid the country of the influence of White man. He would restore the purity of the tribe and its wisdom. (95)

So, these words reveal to us the revolutionary fervour of Kabonyi.

The novelist discusses the Christian faith that contaminates the hills and also portends many signs of sickness in society. Muthoni rebels against the conventional Christian religion. She rebels against her father, a devoted Christian, by accepting the tribal customs.

She, in her attempt to reconcile the ways of tribe with those of her father's faith, sacrifices her life. By practising circumcision, she expresses her feeling of disillusionment at the new religion. She in fact acquires martyrdom. Ngugi comments on her death thus:

> I think a person who undergoes martyrdom is not a loser. In the book . . . the girl is dead but not destroyed. . . . An individual importance is not only the life in this world but also the effect his work is on the other people after he has gone.[1]

This passage throws light on the sacrifice made by Muthoni to preserve the tribal customs.

The Mau Mau movement took place in Kenya between October 1952 and October 1953. It was an armed peasant revolt aimed at getting back the lands given to the White farmers by the White government. It developed into guerilla warfare in the dense jungle areas in the Abodare Mountains and around Mount Kenya just North of Nairobi. About fifteen thousand people, primarily Gikuyu tribesmen, fought in the forest. They were the true freedom fighters who did not keep themselves silent when they were met with injustice. Ngugi writes:

> To most Africans Mau Mau was in fact a heroic and glorious aspect of that mainstream [the mainstream of African Nationalism]. The basic objectives of Mau Mau revolutionaries were to drive out the Europeans. Seize the government and give back to the Kenyan peasants their stolen lands and property.[2]

The colonists and the missionaries felt that Mau Mau war was a threat to Christianity in the form of a new religion. Harry Likey, one of the earliest missionaries, says:

> I am sure now that the Mau Mau was a new religion of which the oath ceremony formed only a small part that was the force which was turning thousands of peace living Gikuyu into murderers and fanatics.[3]

Elspeth Huxley, a spokesperson of the settlers, also expressed the negative estimate of Mau Mau:

> The majority of the Gikuyu feared the Mau Mau leaders as the majority of the Germans feared the Nazis. . . . The Nazis had their concentration camps, their strangling ropes and knives added to this. Mau Mau leaders had behind them the ancient fear of magic which bound those who were forced into submission to keep their oaths.[4]

The White settlers felt that the Africans were returning to the law of the jungle by the Mau Mau organisation whose background was associated with many of the evils of tribal witchcraft. The early British version of Mau Mau runs thus:

> the failure of the Gikuyu to adjust themselves fully to the need the sudden change together with the planned exploitation of the attendant stresses and strains were primary causes and origin of Mau Mau.[5]

These prejudiced views on Mau Mau were opposed by the writers like Ngugi who considered Mau Mau movement an anti-injustice movement and the most glorious aspect of African nationalism.

In his novels, Ngugi sets out to disprove the specific charges made by the colonialist historians. He tries to restore the traditional Gikuyu values. He earnestly feels that the Mau Mau was a political movement with legitimate arms but not an atavistic religion. It consisted of brave and dedicated heroes and not cruel murderers. Ordinary Gikuyu people suffered immensely during the emergency. Ngugi intends to redeem the traditional African culture from the biased view of the colonial historians. In *The River Between*, there is an attempt to reconcile the best of tribal and Christian way to form a viable spiritual guide for the people. The best of the tribal is represented in the character of Chege. He is the preserver of tribal values.

> The other elders feared and respected him or he knew more than any other person the ways of the lands and the hidden things of the tribal. He knows the meaning of every ritual and every sign. So he was at the head of every important ceremony.[6]

Chege is a visionary who has warned his people of the devastative effects of the White man or the unity of the tribe. When they suffered to hear his warnings, he places his faith in his son whom he sends to the missionary school to prepare for the fight against the intruders. Chege's worldview is slowly lost to the tribals. This is indicated in the very moving scene in which Chege takes his son Waiyaki to Mount Kenya, the seat of the tribe's legendary founders, Gikuyu and Mumbi. So, Ngugi's primary concern is the present. The book stresses the cultural continuity rather than strict adherence to past names.

In *The River Between* and *Weep Not, Child*, the protagonists, Waiyaki, Njoroge, Ngotho and Boro expressed their political consciousness. Waiyaki, like a dreamer, has the following vision of education as the universal panacea.

> The idea of education had now come to him like a demon, urging him to go on, do more. . . . He saw only schools, schools everywhere and thirst that burned in the throats of so many children who looked up to him for the quenching water. (98)

In the end, he realises that education has to be for something:

> All at once, Waiyaki realised what the ridges wanted. All at once, he felt more forcibly than he has ever felt before the shame of people's being taken away, the shame of being forced to work on those same lands, the humiliation of paying taxes for a government

> that you knew nothing about. . . . Now he knew what he would preach if he never got another chance; Education for unity. Unity for political freedom. (142-43)

These words of Waiyaki express the harm done by the education system. The African experience in the world is defined and reflected in the European experience of history. Their entire way of looking at the world, even the world of immediate environment was Eurocentric. So he wants to orientate Europeans towards placing Africa in the centre.

> All other things are to be considered in their relevance throughout situation and their contribution towards understanding ourselves . . in suggesting this, we are not rejecting our streams, especially, the western stream. We are all only mapping out the directions and perspectives. The study of culture and literature will inevitably take in an African unity.[7]

Even in *Weep Not, Child*, Njoroge gains the insight on the land. He thinks thus: "The land needed him and God had given him an opening so that he might come back and save his family and the whole country." (119) *But* Njoroge is an unrealistic dreamer who looks forward to some unspecified tomorrow where everything would be fine. His failure lies in substituting the dreams for action. No doubt political action takes place in the novel when Njoroge's brother joins the Mau Mau. They express their revenge and participation in the movement.

Boro who represents angry young generation took Mau Mau oath and fought from the forest to get back their occupied lands. He has gone to the Great War on the side of the Europeans and has come to know the Whites's exploitative ways. He kills the exploiters—White Settler Howlands and the African chief Jacobo. Ngotho waits for a long time to get back his lands as was prophesied by Mugo wa Kabiro. Later he participates in the strike to have wages without any racial discrimination.

In *A Grain of Wheat*, a complete political consciousness is evident in the protagonist. Here, Kihika says: "it is not politics, Wambuku, it is life. Is he a man who lets another take away his land and freedom? Has a slave life?" (85) He acts according to his principles but is betrayed and also killed. He resembles Boro, the revolutionary figure in *Weep Not, Child.* It is Mugo who betrays Kihika. Mugo has both knowledge of political situation and an ability to act, but he makes the wrong choice. Caught by the true opposing forces of the war, Mugo asks himself:

> What shall I do? If I don't serve Kihika he will kill me. . . . If I work for him, the Government will catch him. The White man has long arms. And they will hang me. My God! I don't want to die. (169)

His answer to his question is to betray Kihika to the White. Thus by turning one enemy into a friend and having the other killed, he is able to rid himself of both enemies at the same time.

Kihika stands prominent among the small men and women of the village. He is the young man who sees the vision of an independent Kenya. He knows the heroic tradition of his country. He visualizes himself as "a saint leading the Gikuyu people to freedom and power," (97) and, above all, his role as a new anti-crime, urging his companions to sacrifice themselves to the achievement of the freedom. Kihika sacrifices his life for the sake of his country.

> Kihika was hanged in public, one Sunday, . . . A combined force of Homeguards and Police whipped and drove people from Thabai and other ridges to see the body of the rebel dangling on the tree, and learn. (17)

Karanja searches his heart for pity and for his lost friend. It is not any youthful attempt for Kihika that prevents Karanja to rededicate to the cause of independence. Karanja has a sense of self-preservation struggling in him.

It is Kihika who comes before us as a typical rebel who wages his protest against White settlers. G.D. Killam sees in him "a figure embodying both the values and spirit of independence fighter."[8] Having been brutally tortured and then hanged on a tree, before the novel opens on 'Uhuru' arrangements, Kihika lives on in the minds of the villagers. Towards the White man he hardens or

> long before he has even encountered a White face, and gradually develops a strategy to regain independence. As a boy, he is grounded by the village, in the political history of Kenyan struggle for independence right from the days of Waiyaki. The warrior through Harry Tiku's cursing all the White man's benevolence and protection. (97)

which has denied people, land and freedom to the days of Jomo Kenyatta in whom Kenya sees a redeemer. Hearing about the mission school "that forebodes circumcision in order to eat like insects both the roots on the stem or Gikuyu society" (16), Kihika enters into a squabble with his teacher and runs away from the school to avoid a public shame whipping "ten minutes on his naked buttocks in front of the whole assembly" (101). Out of school Kihika teaches himself how to read, write Swahili and English, goes to work in Nairobi, attends political meetings, discovers the party and finds a new vision. Being in the party, he hears of India and how "the British ate India's wealth. They drank India's blood." (88)

Adept in argument, rude in political judgement, Kihika "turns the language of the Christians on themselves."[9] He feels that Christ failed because his death did not change anything and therefore, he says what is needed in Kenya is a death which will change things, that is to say, "we want a true sacrifice" (95). So he says:

> I die for you, you die for me, we become a sacrifice for one another. So I can say that you, Karanja, are Christ, I am Christ. Everybody who takes the oath of Unity to change things in Kenya is a Christ. (95)

Thus Kihika, the freedom fighter, develops into an extension of Jesus Christ, "a compliment of the saviour of saviours and makes it plain that the struggle was a just one."[10]

A few months after the declaration of Emergency, when all the leaders of land have been arrested and when nobody knows where they have been taken, a day has come for Kihika to choose between prison and forest. He chooses forest and collects a band of fighters, more than three hundred in all. He carries "not mark but a Bible, he knows as intimately as land, he is fighting for."[11] At first rose the Mahi Police post, a symbol of White man's might and one Friday evening finishes the man-eater, Thomas Robson. He, entering Mugo's hut in tears, whispers to him: "I shot him. I have been wanting to finish him all these months." (215)

Kihika believes in the dictum, 'union is strength.' So he tells Mugo:

> A people united in faith are stronger than the warm and in a fight for freedom a few shall die that the many shall live that is what crucifixion means today. (217)

He even tells Mugo that he should organise an underground movement which can be a bridge between the forest fighters and the people in the village. Arranging the place of their next meeting in the forest, he slips out into the dark amidst distant screams of people whose houses are being searched and who are shot at by the police in connection with Robson's death. Unfortunately, Mugo arrives at the office and betrays Kihika, thereby committing treason. In the words of the General, Kihika walks straight into the trap and dies a martyr's death. In the words of Peter Nazareth, Kihika "who is motivated by a powerful desire for justice and refused to compromise in his pursuit of truth and justice"[12] lives on in the minds of the people and influences their deeds.

Kihika never believes the European critics' view that the Africans never protested against the White colonists. He stood prominently among the villagers, saw the vision of an independent Kenya and hoped to lead his people to the 'Promised Land' and died a heroic death through his elegance and glorious actions. His image is felt throughout the novel. The sense of commitment that radiates from the spirit of Kihika proves that he is actually 'the representative consciousness of the Ngugi strong men.'

His rebellious spirit easily finds a place in Ngugi's next novel, *Petals of Blood*, which records the neo-colonial attitude of the Kenyan Karega who with his faith and hope inspires others, becomes a typical hero waging a war against the naked, shameless, direct, brutal exploitation in Kenya. He is

> a typical rebel who tries to restore the Africans their home or of building a new home, a true communal home for all Africans.[13]

Karega emerges as the hero of the novel, the pilgrim who travels through time and space and tries to discover Africa's true past and its meaning. He covers the length and breadth of Kenya looking for a solution to the problems of the toiling masses of Africa.

As a student at Siriana, Keraga organises a strike against Fraudsham, the principal of the school. He demands for an Africanisation of the curriculum and the staff and a more democratic way of running the school. So he sang with hope a new school, a new beginning and a new people. When Chui succeeds Fraudsham, he continues the good old fraudulent methods of Fraudsham. Karega continues his war against the new principal but he is expelled. Even then he sustains his rebellious spirit against the exploiters. Karega disapproves of the lawyer's liberalism in an answer to the problems of the land. He even disregards contemptuously Munira's religious fighting as the means of establishing justice on earth or preparing the self or a future life after death. He believes firmly in the collective struggle as one part of a new world, a new earth. If New Jerusalem is not reached today, Karega feels sure the fighters among the children daily being born will continue to struggle. The novel grippingly celebrates the spirit of struggle of the people's heroes who led such struggle. As a true preserver of African culture and ethos, Karega says:

> The true lesson of history was that the so-called victims, the poor, the downtrodden, the masses had always struggled with spears and arrows with their hands and songs of courage and hope to end their oppression and exploitation: that they would continue their struggling. (303)

In the end, Karega tells that he and his people will struggle until a human kingdom is born. He would like to see a world in which goodness and beauty, strength and courage are seen. Culture and science from all ages and clans would not be the monopoly of a few but for the use of all.

Karega in an hallucinatory dream sums up the history of black man and sees in the current conditions as coincidence with other suppressed people betrayed as in Kenya by their own countrymen.

Karega is Ngugi raisonneur in the novel for the possibility of a New Jerusalem by an appeal to peasantry and workers with the examples of the heroes of other revolutions. Like a typical revolutionary, he asks the peasants to struggle to seize power and overturn the system. Then only would the Kingdom of men and women would begin. The reality out of which Karega's revolution rises is new Illmorog where the highway, the symbol of modernity, the Whites, the village bring to it the chaos of the city, alienates the people from traditional land and creates devisable class struggle.

Like Karega, Abdulla, Wanja, Nyakinyua, and Munira in their own way are revolutionary leaders. Nyakinyua with her power of oratory inspires the Illmorog people and infuses a community spirit in them. Abdulla, who actively aligns himself with the Mau Mau struggle, is incarcerated and released from detention on the eve of 'Uhuru.' "His amputated limb is a physical testimony to the sacrifices which the peasants had to come in struggle for independence."[14] With his courage, integrity and commitment, he shows his readiness to help others in trouble. Throughout the novel, he, with his revolutionary fervour, serves a symbol of struggle and sacrifice.

Wanja, with her own struggle against oppression and exploitation, becomes a rebel in one of the leaders guiding Illmorog people to their M.P., Munira, another leader who with his liberal thinking attempts to link up his genuine religious sensibility with a socialistic principle. Thus these leaders become bitter critics of the neo-colonists and they sincerely attempt to transform the masses into the active agents through their actions. They also draw the attention of their brothers to the economic recession that exacerbated the gulf between the rich and the poor. They prompt their note of revolution by adopting a revolutionary stance. In fact, the villagers express their voice collectively thus:

> We shall not forget Karega and Munira and Abdulla and Wanja and a Donkey . . . they saved us . . . their unselfish involvement in our lives. . . . All this saved us . . . we shall always remember, these heroes in our amidst. (242)

This is further reiterated by Ngugi in his *The Homecoming* where he talks about the results produced by the revolutionaries on the villagers.

> The Kenyan ruling class was martially scared of peasants and workers who showed no fear in their eyes; workers and peasants who showed no submissiveness: workers and peasants who proclaimed with history with unashamed pride who denounced its betrayal with courage. (xix)

This spirit of revolution is further exemplified in *Devil on the Cross*. It is a revolutionary novel in indigenous Kenyan language that reconstructs "the Kenyan people's struggles against the neo-colonial form and the stage of imperialism."[15] It captures the nature of

> Revolution in humanistic context by differentiating the psychological, sociological and unverbalised motives in the working class against the materialistic acquisition—land, property, beliefs and rituals born with the materialistic attitude of the coloniser.[16]

There is an ironic inversion of the story of crucifixion. The devil is crucified by the workers and peasants and then it is taken from the cross and nurtured towards resurrection by the rich and the powerful who live by Satan and prosper as he prospers. Ngugi does this to make the abstract concepts of good and evil so often referred to as opposites, concentric and substantial. There is an authorial voice which represents the peasants and the workers of the village. In keeping with the oral tradition of Africa, there is the use of songs which is integrated in the text. The songs are mostly the perorations of angry peasants and workers of Kenya who become critical of the neo-colonist. Wariinga's cry "Get thee behind me, Satan" (194) shows that she finds a "common ground between socialist humanistic ethics and Christian ethics."[17]

The novel is dedicated to all Kenyans struggling against the neo-colonial stage of imperialism. He introduces the plot and places, the work in the context of an oral tradition, The Devil appeared to Wariinga on one Sunday and told her that it is 'leaping ahead of the story.' The description of her dream illustrates her symbolic revolution. While simultaneously parading the events leading up to and including the passion of Christ, she saw a crowd of people in rags walking in the light propelling the devil towards the cross. One sees the devil that was

> clad in a silk suit and he carried a walking stick shaped like a folding umbrella . . . his belly sagged, as if it were about to give birth to all the evils of world. His skin was red, like that of a pig. (13)

The grotesque elements of this dream and its fright sit recurring on Wariinga's consciousness. Ordinarily, one gives the meaning of the Devil representing all the evils of the world, 'Monopoly Capitalism' which the novelist attacks scathingly. The dominant image results from the yoking together of diametrically opposed symbols (crucifying the Devil is very powerful). As we gather from the Bible, the implication of crucifixion or physical suffering as self-sacrifice to redeem mankind comes of imaginative and spiritual exaltation. But the novelist makes a spurious inversion of the Biblical pattern. Lisa Curtis says:

> the people may be broadly equated with the Roman troops. Judeo and the other dressed in suits and ties who lifted the Devil down from the cross with the followers of the deity. The inversion is complete. Yet such close textual parody of Christ passion necessarily anticipates resurrection. And it is in celebration of the devil risen that the ceremonies at Illmorog are intended.[18]

Set against this thematic framework is the story of Wariinga whose exposure to the realities of modern theft and robbery awaken her social conscience to a kind, religious fervour and realisation that her past helplessness is effectively a silent acquiescence to the stethoscope. Her role in the novel is to demonstrate the birth of a revolutionary conclusiveness which is practical and effective.

As a rebel, Wariinga cannot remain passive and indulge in self-pity while facing the reality of colonisers. Edward W. Syed says:

> If a filial relationship was held together by natural bonds and natural forms of authority—involving obedience, fear, love, respect and instinctual conflict—the new afflictive relationship changes these bonds into what seem to be transpersonal forms such as guilt consciousness, consensus, collegiality, professional respect—class and hegemony of dominant culture. The filial scheme belongs to the realms of nature and life, whereas affiliation belongs to culture and society.[19]

Ngugi's affiliation is to invent signifiers of black cultural consciousness and create a fictional form which reveals the component of this culture-consensus, collegiality and professional respect and its hegemony. Affiliation in this respect becomes "in effect a literal form, the representation by which what is ours is good. And therefore deserves incorporation and inclusion in the programs of humanistic study." (*Ibid.*, 21)

In this novel, the upturning of myth generates fear, unrest and violence which trouble Ngugi's mind to the extent that he must bring about the solution to his people by writing about the combat of the two cultures against the self-destruction of the class he affiliates with. Naturally, he shares with Frantz Fanon who says:

> This idea of clandestine culture is immediately seen in the reaction of the occupying pace which interprets attachment to traditions as faithfulness to the spirit of the nation as a refusal to submit. This persistence in following forms of culture which are already condemned to extension is already a demonstration which is thrown back to the laws of inertia. There is no taking of offensive and no redefining of relationship.[20]

Wariinga's initial dream in fear, her transformation as a worker, her fight with the car owner who would molest her body while she is working his engine, her killing of her seducer while the wedding bells are ringing, demonstrate this 'throw back inertia' of her cultural humanity.

The novelist needs to show the combat, this 'throw back inertia' in his narrative power in the gathering force of the first fearful dream of Wariinga. Here, the motives are still of the oppressed, of the growing ferocity of the revenge for humanistic climatic movements which should awaken at least the terror-stricken humanity of the oppressor too. Since, the novelist lives in the self-contained moments of bottled up cultural humanity which comes out destructively anyway, he needs to tell the ghostly story to invest at least the possibilities of humanism in the hearts of the colonists who have immersed themselves in the native culture with which even possibilities allow them. What the novelist, as a critic, does in this novel is to show what his guide Frantz Fanon has already suggested:

> it is the literature of combat, because it moulds the natural consciousness giving it a form and contours and flinging open before it new and boundless horizons; it is literature of combat because it assumes responsibility and because it is the will to liberty expressed in terms of time and space. (193)

The fearful dream about *Devil on the Cross* and to its actualisation throughout the novel and Wariinga's encounters and an exhibition of her rebellious spirit pervade the novel.

In the very opening of the novel, the authorial voice involves the spirit of the place and races to question and exposes the people who wronged its inhabitants.

> And then Wariinga's mother came to me when dawn was breaking, and in tears she beseeched me; Gicaandi player, tell the story of the child I loved so dearly. Cast light upon all that happened so that each may pass judgement only when he knows the whole truth. (7)

The authorial voice becomes a judicial critic within the form of fictional discourse. And then with the reader "come let us reason together . . . about Jacinta Wariinga before you pass judgement on our children" (9). The novelist brings out the simultaneity of the whole situation through the revolutionary 'spirit of the place' which forms Kenya's two cities—Nairobi and Illmorog. The dream of hatred envelops everything she builds up. Her physique, her affiliation with black Kenyans and its women shocked that her betrothed father was the Rich Old Man who seduced her. She realises that she cannot have 'separate peace' from her people. In her dream, she saw,

> first the darkness, carved open at one side to reveal a Cross which hung in the air. Then she saw a crowd of people dressed in the rags propelling the Devil towards the Cross . . . you encourage lasciviousness solely to gratify your appetite . . . you seize men's wealth, then you dress in robes of friendship and instruct them to join in the pursuit of the villain who has robbed them. (13)

The grotesque element of this dream and its frights recur on the consciousness of Wariinga. She thinks of her childhood and of Rich Old Man of Ngorika who makes her pregnant, her boss, John Kimwana, who dismisses her from the job of secretary. Like a typical rebel, she expresses her anger with a conviction:

> You snatcher of other people's lives? Do you remember the game you and I used to play, the game of the hunter and the hunted. Did you imagine that the day might come when the hunted would become the hunter. What is done cannot be undone. I am not going to save you. But I shall save many other people whose lives will not be ruined by words of honey and perfume. (253)

These lines express the rebellious spirit of Wariinga, particularly in doing away the ills in the Kenyan society. Thus she becomes a staunch revolutionary attacking the betrayals of African aspirations following political independence.

Wariinga's present condemnation to innocence results from her childhood's seduction, which reflects in the nightmare after she loses her job in Nairobi. She needs to recover from it. The first initiative she takes is to assert and break the self-shield of fear. She insists the driver to drive even when she is the only passenger. When a couple more join in, she gains confidence. The little experience of asserting herself makes her very active. Wariinga rejects the materialistic worldly wisdom of Satan. It is the wealthy and the socially complacent who left the devil from the cross. The novelist sees the vast congregation of the pseudo-

Christians of the world in Africa as using their religion as a cynical frontage to conceive their self-seeking opportunism. Like almost every member of the gathering in the cave, the Rich Old Man is a pillar of his sect. When Wariinga enquires where he intends to grow through a form of marriage with her as his second wife, he reminds her: "I am a man of the Church. I just want you to be mine. I will find my own ways of coming to visit you" (253). The authorial voice runs thus:

> You ask what has been stolen from Muthuri. Aren't his sweat and blood worth anything? Where did you teach the wealth of nation comes from? From the clouds? From the hands of the rich. (186)

The voice becomes very rebellious and says:

> Kineenderi will show them only two worlds, that of the eater and that of the eaten. So, the worker will never learn of the existence of the third world, the world of the revolutionary overthrow of the system of eating and being eaten. They will always assume that the two worlds of the eater and the eaten are eternal. (188)

This voice exposes the precise methods of the power elite and their cynical exploitation of religion as well as some of the anomalies in it.

The voice tries to ensure Wariinga into submission to worldly wisdom. But Wariinga has her work cut out to convince herself later that this was the father of the 'lives speaking' and not 'prophetic spokesmen of humanity.' She utters,

> No. I had been the voice of Satan, the voice of temptation. For although the voice has painted the true picture of what is going on in the country and it has made pertinent observations about neo-colonial Kenya, the way that the voice had shown her as an escape from the prison of neo-colonial life was misleading and would have cost Wariinga her life. It had tempted her to walk along the broad highway carpeted with the flowers of self-seeking individualism. It has tempted her to send her body for money again. (188)

The novel convinces that there is a need for revolution. In the end, revolution itself becomes an alternative religion. Taking over the very vocabulary of the old religion, Muthuri tells Wariinga that he belongs to an order that has been called to serve the people of Kenya. He continues:

> Mau Mau has passed on its tradition of communal self-help. If we don't help each other we will become like beasts. That is why in the days of Mau Mau we took the oath swearing 'I will never eat alone' . . . work is life. Alliance sanctified the Holy Trinity of the worker, the peasant and the patriot. (230)

Like Karega, Muthuri suffers for his efforts in going about to rouse consciousness of the workers and rally them to stand up for their rights. But the profits of the employers increase at the same rate as increase in prices—in fact, sometimes the rate of profit is higher than the price increase. So when the price of things goes up, the employer is benefitted; but a lot of the workers get worse. The novelist very much wants that triumphant march of the Holy Trinity which sets the power group by the heels. On the workers' behalf, one of the workers expresses his protest:

> What about us the workers. We build houses. Others occupy them and we, the builders, are left in rain. We make clothes. Others take them and dress. We the tailors go naked. We grow food, others eat it and we the farmers sleep without stomachs growling through the height. Look here, we built good schools. Other people's children find places in them and ours go looking for food in rubbish heaps and in dustbins. Today, we are taking a stand. Today here we refuse to go on being the pot that cooks but never tastes the food.[21]

This passage expresses the wild protest of the peasants, the workers and the students of Kenya.

The novelist asks the reader to choose between the good and the evil forces. He says:

> Heaven and hell? Both exist. There is a difference between them just as there is a difference between good and evil. A good heart and an evil heart. Listen! Our lives are a battlefield on which is fought a continuous war between the forces that are pledged to confirm our humanity and those determined to dismantle it.[22]

In this battle, Wariinga takes the side of the forces of making her humanity grow. Gaturia makes an active attempt to break away from the pretty bourgeoisie intellectual and from their hypocritical mortal tenure of progressive class politics at the university. In this sneer attempt to reject those 'life lies,' Gaturia offers a model for a deeply alienated youth of today. In the end, Wariinga chooses her side and transforms her way of life. Simon Gikandi comments:

> This Wariinga is not the one who uses to think that there was nothing that she could do except type for others. The one who used to burn her body with 'Umbi' and 'Snownfire' to change the colour of her skin to please her eyes, to satisfy their lust for White skins. The one who used to think that there was only one way of avoiding the pitfalls of life: suicide.[23]

Thus one notices the process of metamorphosis in her from a typist to a potentially ideal young revolutionary woman.

Wariinga is fitted to her task of shooting the rich. She speaks like people's judge about to deliver his judgement. She shoots the rich old man who is the representative of all the licentious, arrogantly selfish and utterly materialistic hypocrites who dominate the society so fiercely indicted by the novelist. In this act, she is "the deliberate, competent, fearless and heroine of toil."[24]

Wariinga grows into an idealised figure of revolutionary womanhood. She has trained as an auto-engineer, the hard way. She has gone to evening classes in Karate and can defend herself against her personal assault. She is a worker among workers and her individual triumph does not alter the society. But she has expressed her voice against a destructive solid system backed by ruthlessly well-armed and legalized forces of protection.

Like a typical rebel, Wariinga makes use of gun to transform the society around her. With the aid of the gun, she will improve an inexorable moral code. She salvages her honour by righteously condemning her elitist persecutor to death. Tomorrow the persecution of the whole society is to be set right by armed insurrection. Wariinga is tuned to act. She does unhesitatingly as an instrument of nemesis. She guns down the rich old man as a retribution for the social evil he epitomises. The revolutionary wrath of Wariinga takes revenge upon the gang of exploiters and other henchmen. Thus, she encounters the unjust forces and stands as a true rebel in the novel.

The novel presents the nature of revolution in humanistic context by differentiating the psychological, sociological and unverbalised motives in the working class against materialistic acquisition. Ngugi becomes a satiric critic of contemporary Kenya against a vision of socialistic Kenya purged of neo-colonialism.

This rebellion of novel recurs in the novel *Matigari*. The word Matigari in Gikuyu means 'the remnants.' The novel was originally written in Gikuyu with a view to reaching Kenyans. Any leftovers of food or dregs in drinks became a signifier of Mau Mau, which functioned as a trope mediating the colonial past and the postcolonial movement. Now Matigari represents an attempt to celebrate the once unmentioned Mau Mau and to introduce it into the political vocabulary of Kenya. Unfortunately, Mau Mau could not be incorporated in full into the postcolonial's power knowledge configuration because the men who had inherited colonial power had been some of its opponents. The figure in Ngugi's novel refers to General Stanley Mathenge who had left the Nyandarua mountains in the mid-1950s and reached Ethiopia. Mathenge was unhappy with what was going on in the postcolonial Kenya and in fact he was waiting for an appropriate time to return and restore the reign of justice and truth. So Ngugi's fictional Matigari is a typical fictional character who posed a palpable threat to the Kenyan political establishment. So in this novel it is Matigari who hopes to "transcend the materiality of state power and neo-colonialism. (131)

The novel created a stir in Kenya. It seeks "to initiate a public debate about issues that the authorities prefer to restrict to academic seminars and conferences." (161)

The presence of the hero Matigari was felt everywhere but the government was very much perturbed that they discovered in the end that Matigari was a fictional character and so they set out to destroy the book that had promoted his presence. Matigari comes before us as a rebel who asks questions and creates conditions which undermine the political system's ecumenical discourse of power.

Matigari becomes a representative of Ngugian rebels who feels that the nature of struggle is unequivocal. He also asserts that those who sow the seeds must reap the fruits. He earnestly feels that White settlers and black authorities represent western capitalism. He ultimately repudiates any route to liberation that falls short of an armed uprising. He says, "the enemy can never be driven out by words alone, no matter how sound the argument" (138). He continues his rebellious spirit by implacably articulating thus: "Justice for the oppressed comes from a sharpened sphere" (131) and again "Justice for the oppressed springs from the armed might of the united dispossessed" (161). This is the rebellious spirit sustained by Matigari.

Matigari, like other freedom fighters, fought for the independence of Kenya. After the independence, he left the forest and buried his guns and his sword under a wild fig tree and put on the belt of peace because he believed that the end of fighting meant the end of injustice. Soon he discovers that the land through which he travels suffers from a great heat that symbolises the endemic oppression in the demoralised land. He comes to know that injustice still exists in the neo-colonial society. The White men against whom he fought have been replaced by their sons who now have become partners in 'reaping what they did not sow.'

Matigari, during his quest, encounters quite a few allegoric figures including the boy Muriuki and the young woman Guthera, the absurd and sinister minister for Truth and Justice, the worker leader Ngaruro wa Kiriro, the people and the police. There is an allusion to Matigari's Christ-like commitment to the truth despite the Makari violence and threat of death with which he is surrounded. He rescues the young prostitute Guthera from two policemen who have been pursuing her. They set their dogs on her, thereby asserting their oppressive function as instruments of authority and also a metaphor for the brutality of their lust. Guthera confesses to her rescuer. Her story is one of the extreme innocence and of religious passion perverted by corrupt and irresponsible men. If the reborn Guthera can be regarded as pure, the lost boy Muriuki is resurrected. The corruption of the adult world is evident in Muriuki's story which is the same as Guthera's experience. Matigari rescues them.

Matigari continues his rebellious spirit. But he is imprisoned when he tries to expel the people who occupy the house built by him and his children. In the prison he divides his food and drink among the other prisoners. He inspires the inmates by quoting from the Bible,

> and when the time for the supper came, he sat at the table together with the disciples. He told them I want you to share this last supper with me, to remind us that we shall not be able to eat together again unless our kingdom comes. (57)

Matigari escapes from jail boldly. He brandishes a flaming sword and the doors are opened. He has a voice like thunder and when he speaks, smoke gushes from his mouth. Within three days after his arrest, he walks out of the jail boldly. When he appears before the people, they reject him as a mad man and drunkard. Troubled by his failure to convince others to accept his vision, Matigari goes into the wilderness where he interprets his failure in terms of an ancient natural wisdom and mourns for the day when people could still read the stars.

Matigari makes a final attempt to convince the people. He approaches a student, a teacher and a priest. Unfortunately, all fail abysmally. Their denial of Matigari condemns them as irresolute and complicit with the oppression. The minister of Truth and Justice appeals to the factory works to end their strike at the factory. He tries to silence the workers through bullets and power.

Matigari understands that his attempts at peaceful change have failed, so he takes up his guns. He has no choice but to fight. His experience and sacrifice give him authority to speak for the victims of oppression. The people also supposedly grant him unimpeachable integrity in his stand against the oppressor for no other perspective carries any weight against his own. He asks the masses thus: "what other deed do you need that is greater than the blood I shed?" (50) In the end he gives his life for the land. According to him there are only two types of people in the land—patriots and traitors.

As a rebel, Matigari expresses his displeasure at the degraded women. He sees women who are 'either fat, gossipy creatures who work in bars or frivolous individuals like the wife of the minister of Truth and Justice whose most noticeable act is to sleep with the chauffeur in the back seat of her black Mercedes. Guthera is depicted as the beautiful, rare and pure seeming woman who is nevertheless available. She is depicted as 'wrongly in prostitution.' Muriuki and Guthera declare themselves child and wife to Matigari, subordinating them joyfully to him as the noble patriarch.

Matigari frightened the government of Kenya who searched for him but in the end found out that he was only a fictional character created by Ngugi. They confiscated all the copies of it. As a rebel he threatened the Kenyan government in the postcolonial era.

Through the use of the Christian liberalism the novelist takes us to the world of radical socialism which imbricates with cultural nationalism. Matigari is a Christ-like figure. He has resurrected Christ's ability to appear and disappear at will. He has a superhuman ability to go on without food or drink and not to tire. He leaves behind the paths walked by the people. He goes into the wilderness. Finally he escapes, unseen, through the window of a burning house completely surrounded by the police. It is clearly a miracle which the 'assembled crowd' has gathered to witness. The lightening and the peal of thunder which rend the sky are obviously reminiscent of gospels account of Jesus's death. Ngugi imitates the Bible only to reinvigorate the commitment to a specific political and historical context. The process of contextualising religious ritual is then immediately carried forward to a tradition of communalism.

> Great love I sow there
> Among the women and the children.
> When a bean fell,
> We would share it among ourselves. (55-56)

These lines on one level remind us of the Biblical notion of sharing the food with others but they overtly express the rebellious spirit of Matigari of sharing food with his comrades. So one finds "an unmistakable synchronizing of Christian ritual with a political appropriation of traditional ritual."[25]

Matigari with his Christian teaching comes out with his quest for truth and justice

> Look! See the Boys and the Williamses coming to you. Please send them away and have them thrown into the everlasting fire you made for the likes of imperialists and their overseers. For you were hungry, but they gave you no food: you were thirsty and they gave you no water: you are naked, but they clothed you not. (81)

These lines reveal to us the rebellious spirit of Matigari.

Matigari easily becomes a representative of the Kenyan workers. He identifies himself with the peasants. He continues his address to the Kenyan peasants and workers.

> Imperialism has tried to kill that God within us. But one day that God will return from the dead . . . and liberate us who believe in Him. But . . . if you let the country go to the imperialist enemy and its local watchdogs, it is the same thing as killing that God who is inside you. (156)

Here Matigari insists on the Christ-like nature of the Kenyan dispossessed in the interest of fostering resistance to that dispossession. He is putting the Biblical terms towards a socialist revolution. Matigari asks the individual members of working class and peasants to wage a war against the oppressors. He even draws their attention to mass political action. Thus Matigari asks his people to continue 'the tradition of struggle for political and economic freedom' given by the land and freedom army in the 1950s, backed by traditions of both peasant revolt and nationalistic politics extending back to the 1920s and continued upto the peasant movement such as Mwakenya.

Early strikes against the peasant's alienation from their lands, the Mau Mau movement, the revolt against the elite Africans who follow the values of the Whites in the post-Independence era etc.—all are portrayed grippingly in Ngugi's novels mainly to refuse the Eurocentric view that the Kenyans submitted themselves meekly before the Whites. Ngugi sincerely believes that the use of violence to preserve the oppressive social order always diminishes man but he is purified when it is used to change the unjust social order. Besides advocating protest and resistance, Ngugi, in his novels emphasizes the need for Kenyans to grow as worthy individuals and good citizens to build up a better nation.

NOTES

1. Robert Serumage, "A Mirror of Integration: Chinua Achebe and James Ngugi," *Protest and Conflict in African Literature*, ed. Cosmo Pieterse and Donald Munru (New York: Publishing Corp. (1969), p. 75.
2. Ngugi wa Thiong'o, *Homecoming* (London: Heinemann, 1972), p. 28.
3. Harry Likey, *Defeating Mau Mau* (London: Methuen, 1954), pp. 42-43.
4. Elspeth Huxley and Marjorie Perham, *Race and Politics in Kenya* (London: Faber and Faber, 1944), pp. 257-58.
5. *The Manchester Guardian*, 30 October 1952.
6. Christian Hotst Peterson, "Birth Pangs of a National Consciousness: Mau Mau and Ngugi," *WLWE*, Vol. 20, No. 2 (Autumn 1981), p. 217.
7. Ngugi wa Thiong'o, *Homecoming*, p. 146.
8. G.D. Killam, *An Introduction to the Writings of Ngugi wa Thiong'o* (London: Heinemann, 1980), p. 28.
9. *Ibid.*, p. 59.
10. *Ibid.*, p. 53.
11. Adrean Roscoe, *Uhuru's Fire* (Cambridge: Cambridge University Press, 1972), p. 72.
12. Peter Nazereth, "Is *A Grain of Wheat* a Socialist Novel?" *Literature and Society in Modern Africa: Essays on Literature* (Nairobi: East African Literature Bureau, 1972) p. 144.
13. Ngugi, *Homecoming*, xix.
14. Chidi Amuta, *The Theory of African Literature: Implications for Practical Criticism* (London: 2 ED Books, 1989), p. 146.

15. Ngugi wa Thiong'o, *Detained: A Writer's Prison Dairy* (London: Heinemann, 1981), p. 14.
16. Davender Mohan, "Semiology Wariinga's Dream in Ngugi's *Devil on the Cross*," *Commonwealth Fiction*, Vol. 2, p. 206.
17. David Cook, *Ngugi wa Thiong'o: An Exploration of his Writings* (London: Heinemann, 1983), p. 131.
18. Lisa Curtis, "The Divergence of Art and Ideology in the Later Novels of Ngugi" *UFAHAMU*, Vol. 6, No. 2-3 (1984), p. 211.
19. Edeard W. Syed, *The World, the Test and the Critic* (London: Faber and Faber, 1984), p. 20.
20. Frantz Fanon, *The Wretched of the Earth* (Harmondsworth: Penguin, 1967), p. 191.
21. Ngugi, *Detained*, p. 3.
22. Coral M. Sicherman, "Ngugi and the Writings of Kenyan History," *RAL*, Vol. 20, No. 3 (1980), p. 380.
23. Simon Gikandi, "The Epistemology of Translation: Ngugi's Matigari and Politics of Language," *RAF*, Vol.22. No.1 (1991), p. 165.
24. Abdul Razak Gurnah, "Matigari: A tract of resistance," *RAL*, Vol. 22, No. 1 (1991), p. 169.
25. David Maughan Brown, "Matigari and the Rehabilitation of Religion, *RAL*, Vol. 22, No. 1 (1991), p. 176.

Chapter 7

Conclusion

The writers from Commonwealth countries have produced a good body of literature that is being read with considerable respect all over the world. Of the literatures that emanate from the commonwealth, the literature of Africa, has come into literary foreground for total and informed comprehension.

> It is only a generation that the Africa of popular imagination and a wild belief of Africa was created by Rider Haggard and Edgar Wallace and Edgar Rice Burroughs . . . where real was attempted . . . the picture was often a child like race controlled by a superior one. Pseudo scientific myths (the less brain power, sexual prowess) were and still are current.[1]

Africa in the eye of Europe has remained a Dark Continent from Prince Henry, the navigator in the fifteenth century, to the beginning of the twentieth century. In the eighteenth century, the Africans were considered to be in 'a state of nature, in perfect harmony with their environment.' Africa in the eyes of the Europeans remained a 'dark continent' for a long time.

Regarding the debate about the human status of the Africans, a similar image prevailed for a long time. The Africans are called 'noble savages,' 'deprived cannibals,' 'children of nature' and so on. According to the Linnaean classification, the black coloured ones were considered inferior to other races like the whites and the reds. Various kinds of race theories joined to prove too strong the myth of the slave. To the north of the African continent lies the great Sahara desert which separates it from the European land. So it was difficult to enter Africa in those days. Nevertheless, several explorers and traders went round the African continent and touched the land. The vast coastal line of the African continent had been known since a long time. Till the eighteenth century, the Europeans and the Arabs established their castles on the long coastline and traded from there. The traders in the early eleventh century itself established their routes that were stretched till northern Kenya. They collected gold, ivory and above all slaves from Africa and then established the line of commercial exploitation.

In the seventeenth and eighteenth centuries when slave trade was in progress, the Africans were 'noble savages' in European economic terms. In the nineteenth century, the British built up paramountcy on Kenya. During this time 'foreign merchants,' 'concession seekers' and 'moneylenders' were permitted to exploit the economy in Kenya. With the penetration of the Britishers into the interiors of Kenya, the export trade in slaves decreased a little. But the trade in ivory grew year after year. The slave trade and also the ivory had a devastating effect on the Africans in general and the Kenyans in particular. It affected the economic and social conditions of Kenya.

Colonialism undermined the African culture, their religion, education, literature on the one hand and consciously elevated the English language on the other. So the written language in a child's upbringing in the school became divorced from his spoken language at home. There wasn't any relationship between the child's written world, which was also the language of his schooling, and the world of his immediate environment in the family and the community. For a colonial child, the harmonious adjusting between the three aspects of language as communication was completely broken. This resulted in the dissociation of the sensibility of the child from his natural and social environment, in other words, colonial alienation. This alienation became reinforced in the teaching of history, geography, and music where bourgeois Europe was always at the centre of the universe.

In the field of education expansion was made. The physical violence of the battlefield was followed by the psychological violence of the classroom. Cheikh Hamidor Kane describes the situation thus:

> On the black continent one began to understand their real power resided not at all in the cannon of the first morning but in what followed the cannons. Therefore, behind the cannons was the new school. The new school had the nature of both the cannon and the magnet. From the cannon, it took the efficiency of a fighting weapon. But better than the cannon was made the consequent permanent. The cannon forced the body and the school fascinated the soul.[2]

These lines show that the colonists took the Africans further and further from themselves to other selves, from their world to other worlds.

Even with the emancipation of the Africans from the colonialists in the Sixties did not improve the matters in Africa. Unfortunately, the imperialist tradition is maintained in Africa by the international bourgeois using multinational and the flag-waving native ruling classes.

The economic and political dependence of the African neo-colonial bourgeois apemanship and parrotry enforced on a restive operation through police group's barbed wires, a gowned clergy and judiciary. Their ideas were spread by a corpus of state intellectuals, the academic and the journalistic laurels of neo-colonial establishment. To put it in a nutshell, the political independence has not brought true independence as the postcolonial mind still engages itself the colonial experience.

In Africa, oral literature flourished in the past. This 'orature' has been transmitted from one generation to the other. The culture of African society embodies the moral, ethical and aesthetic values through which they come to view themselves and their place in universe. Their values are the basis of their identity, their sense of particularity as members of the human ways. Their language carries all this. Language as culture is the collective memory bank of a people's experience in history. Culture is almost indistinguishable from the language and it makes possible its genesis, growth, articulation and, indeed, its transmission from one generation to the next. The colonists controlled the African culture, thereby controlling the rules of self-definition in relation to others. In Africa, a rich cultural tradition would have absorbed the impact of western culture. Unfortunately, the whites denied the Africans access to progress and systematically sought to destroy this cultural tradition. This resulted in the Africans' facing temporal dispossession. Certain Africans succeeded in asserting to their leaders both at home and abroad that they had enough creative resources to fight away the threat of the dispossession.

The African writers journey, therefore, from the past to the future. They in their works have looked at the history of Africa or the Africans in the last few centuries with a critical eye and have offered a correct perspective of their land and culture. The history in their works is not only of enslavement, brutality, harassment and humiliation but also of a continuous struggle and assertion. History in their works becomes a deeper confrontation with their works, with their own selves and also with the other selves. The works created from the perspective of the struggle of the people dramatize historical moments. They focus on those critical moments when events have seemed to loom larger than any individual. Writers like Ngugi, Rubadire and Hussain Ntheru focused the African ethos and the infrastructure of African social life. Of these, Ngugi comes before us as the first Anglophone African writer who in unambiguous terms puts forth African heritage. He also depicts to the reading public, the historical fact of colonisation and its far-reaching consequences in his country.

Ngugi was born to parents who lost their lands and so he was brought up in an unsafe environment and discomfiture. His secondary education from Alliance High School and collegiate education from Makerere University College never made him comfortable. At the University, he was unhappy because the education system there never allowed the students 'to question them' or compare western institutions with other systems. Writers and thinkers like Lawrence and Conrad bore a deep impress on him. When he was reading Lawrence, he felt the spirituality of things very near him and that he was touching the very spirit of things. The accumulated 'guilt of the colonised' that obtains in the works of Conrad impressed him a lot. During his student days, he contributed his articles to *Pen Point*, a journal of the college. In them, he tried to formulate a definition of African culture and African ethos.

During his stay in England, Ngugi mingled with many young radicals, notably in the group led by Allan Haunt and Arnold Kettle. After obtaining a Masters Degree at Leeds University, he joined as a lecturer at the University College in Nairobi. His zealous proposal of the abolition of the English Department and also of starting a Department of African Literature and Languages did not yield any fruit. So he resigned his lectureship and went to the United States, where he devoted considerable time to creative writing. After coming back from the United States, he joined the Department of English at the University of Nairobi and decided to inspire the people with his creative writings.

Frantz Fanon, Jomo Kenyatta, Peter Abrahams and the Mau Mau movement influenced Ngugi considerably. As a creative writer, he set out to disapprove of the specific charges made by the white historians. He thought that he should restore the Gikuyu values and redeem the Mau Mau movement. He decided that he should write revolutionary works and arouse national consciousness in Kenya.

Ngugi is a fairly prolific writer. Though he has plays, short stories and essays to his credit, he is primarily known to the world for his fictional works. The general political awakening in the country inspired him. He drew his stamina from the peasantry. When he came to know that the comprador section assumed political ascendancy and strengthened economic links with imperialism in what was clearly a neo-colonial arrangement, he became more critical and bitter in his works. He felt that with utmost clarity and varying details of emphasis, he should present in his works, the post-Independence betrayal of hope.

Ngugi wrote in Gikuyu language as his post anti-imperialist struggle of Kenya and African people. He was very sorry to note that in schools and university the African languages were associated with negative qualities of backwardness, underdevelopment, humiliation and punishment. He also noticed with utmost agony, that the people who went through the neo-colonial section and others did not like them. As a typical representative of African ethos and African culture, he thought that the African child should understand his environment in full so as to enable him acquire the capacity to change it for the collective good. The system should record the societal struggle with nature. He felt deeply that an African writer must record people's anti-imperialist struggle to liberate their productive forces from foreign control. It must also have the content for the need for unity among the workers and peasants of all nationalities in their struggle to control the wealth they produce and to free from internal and external parasites. In other words,

> Writers in African languages should reconnect themselves to the revolutionary traditions of an organised peasantry and working class in Africa in their struggle to defeat imperialism and create a higher system of democracy and solidarity in allowance with all the other people of the world. Unity in that struggle would ensure in our multi-lingual diversity.[3]

These lines exhibit how Ngugi would like to record the exploitative public events that have happened around him and their effect on the lives of the individual members of the community. He would like to delineate vividly the history of exploitation of the Africans by the whites and the consequential crippling of such exploitation on the lives of the Africans.

Ngugi discusses the exploitation of the Africans by the British on the basis of race and class in the colonial context. He talks about the crippling effect of the colonial domination in Africa. White missionaries, white settlers and white administrators were the three arms of European power that exploited the natives. It was the missionaries who first came and grabbed the land and then used the power to control by opening schools in the European style. The settlers who followed them with the so-called aid took advantage of the naivete and ignorance of the people and grabbed more lands. Soon it was seen that the new landless peasants were made to work on the land which they had once in their sway and control. The whites ruled them and the whole country. The novelist traces its roots deep down in the psychological, ideological and cultural disintegration in the lives of the Kenyans. He shows how the Kenyans are exploited economically, politically and culturally.

In *The River Between*, Ngugi describes at length the impenetrable Kenya in all its beauty and points out that the Kenyans have been without any fear of invasion by any stranger. They even believed that the land on which they lived was God Murunga's gift to their first parents—Gikuyu and Mumbi. The novelist uses this as the pivot and shows systematically how the usurpers, after driving the people away from their land, try to destroy their cultural heritage and shake the roots of Africa. The arrival of the white man had attacked the rights of the Kenyans, condemned their rituals like circumcision. Livingstone, the head of Siriana missionary and his men started spreading the doctrines of Christianity and laughed at the Gikuyu God by calling him 'the Prince of Darkness.' The effect of such preaching was so much that the early converts like Joshua abandoned their traditional ways in favour of the new faith. Livingstone and his missionary men used Joshua as their agent to preach to the Kenyans to believe in the Bible and give up their native traditions. The act of conversion is the first step of colonialism.

Siriana missionary also started a school to advance the interests of the British Empire. The products of this school are mostly portrayed as misfits in the early colonial period. Waiyaki in *The River Between*, Njoroge in *Weep Not, Child* and Munira in *Petals of Blood*, who received education at Siriana missionary school realised that this education had made them cowards and misfits in their own society. This school during neo-colonial period also produced corrupt officials like Chui and Nderi in *Petals of Blood*. Siriana has paved the way to

> most recent alienation of land here. Siriana forcing many people to move from places they lived in for ages, while others had to live on the same land, working for their new masters. (*RB*, 62)

What is hinted at in *The River Between* is clearly portrayed in the next novel *Weep Not, Child.* This novel clearly brings out the atrocities of the exploiters—usurping the natives' land, turning the African peasants into 'ahois' under the weakened economic conditions, ruthless suppression of their early revolts, the white settlers' materialistic outlook, the African devotion to the ancestral lands, the most inhumanistic suppressive attitude adopted by the whites during the emergency, the physical and psychological effects of such oppression on individuals and society at large. Njeri in this novel describes how the whites exploit the Africans through their draconian laws,

> The white man makes a law or a rule. Through that rule or law . . . he takes away the land. . . . Now that man is taken by the same people who made the laws against which that man was fighting. He is tried under those alien rules. Now tell me who is that man who can win even if the angels of God were his lawyers. (84-85)

Ngotho and his family members, who are suppressed under such oppressive laws by the white settler Howlands, become the representatives of the Africans who have been battered by the colonial exploiters.

A Grain of Wheat, though describes ostensibly the 'uhuru' celebrations, portrays the exploitation, oppression and sufferings of the Africans at the hands of the Europeans just before independence and after independence. The confiscation of the lands through oppressive laws, the most inhumanistic suppression of the detainees, the oppression of the natives, the economic suppression of the workers on the farms during the emergency at its peak are drawn in detail. The psychological effect of suppression at detention camps on the Africans even after their return is portrayed in detail. In a nutshell, Karega says about the exploitation of the Africans by the Europeans in the *Petals of Blood*:

> In the beginning he had the land, the mind and the soul together. On the second day, they took the body away to barter it for silver coins. On the third day, seeing that he was still fighting back, they brought priests and educators to bind his mind and soul so that

> these foreigners could more easily take his land and its produce. (236)

The exploitation of the Africans by the Europeans continues even after Kenya has attained independence. This is portrayed powerfully in his three later novels—*Petals of Blood*, *Devil on the Cross* and *Matigari*.

In *Petals of Blood*, Ngugi impressively presents how the lives of the dispossessed Africans are also broken by an imported capitalist system. It also portrays the religious, political and economic exploiters who swarm upon Illmorog to 'develop' it and use such devices as foreclosed loans to eventually dispossess the local inhabitants. The ruthlessly deprived ordinary people at the hands of the whites are further stripped off at the hands of the corrupt neo-colonial rulers.

Even in *Devil on the Cross*, a research student feels sorry for he has ignored the ancestor's wisdom and philosophy. Like others, he feels that songs, riddles, customs and traditions of the Africans have been totally ignored. Even in *Matigari*, there are references to the atrocious actions of the British settler, John Williams who occupied the natives' land and exploited the African labour.

Exploitation of the Africans by their own countrymen in the colonial and neo-colonial Kenya has been clearly brought out by Ngugi. The Africans who have been set on their own race by the British have proved themselves crueller than their British masters. They act as agents of the British in exploiting their own people for their materialistic gains. They are at once the exploited as well as the exploiters. In *The River Between*, the novelist through Joshua shows how the early converts, in an attempt to prove how good Christians they are, try to suppress mercilessly their traditions and customs. He not only indulges in the cultural exploitation of the natives but also brings divisions in the ridges. In *The River Between*, a group of people on the pretext of upholding the native traditions exploit the innocent public for their personal gains.

In *Weep Not, Child*, the African landowner Jacobo, an agent of the white settler Howlands, supplies African labourers at low wages to work on the settler's fields. In return, he alone grows cash crops like Pyrethium and hinders other Africans from growing it with Howlands help. When he is raised to the power of chief, he tries to suppress Ngotho, an 'Ahoi' and his 'family members' cruelly.

In *A Grain of Wheat*, Karega, Mugo and Gikonyo indulge in the exploitation of the Africans. Mugo hands over the great leader of Mau Mau to the Europeans. Karega becomes a home-guard and exploits his fellow countrymen cruelly. Gikonyo follows capitalist ways to accumulate money and becomes exploiter in the later part of the novel. Africans in the form of homeguards are portrayed as ruthless exploiters in the novel. In this novel, the weakness of the African exploiters is drawn clearly.

In Ngugi's novels—*Petals of Blood, Devil on the Cross* and *Matigari*, the African elite who have adopted the Europeans' ways in exploiting the Africans have been subjected to a critical study. Mounting corruption, insatiable greed for power, relentless means—fair or foul—to quick accumulation of wealth, sharp decline in moral values, unbridled violence—all leading to the utter disillusionment among the Africans during the post independent period are grippingly portrayed in the last three novels.

Unlike many African writers, Ngugi gives prominence to the portrayal of exploited and suppressed African women in the colonial and the neo-colonial Kenya in all his novels. In spite of being brave and independent, all his women characters become victims of exploitation either directly or indirectly on the basis of race, class and gender.

In *The River Between*, Muthoni and Nyambura become victims of cultural exploitation in the clashes between the adventing Europeans with their religion and the resisting Kenyans. Miriamu as wife of pro-Christian leader Joshua suffers during the time of cultural exploitation. In *Weep Not, Child*, Njeri, Nyokobi suffer under the economic suppression during the reign of the White Settler. They also suffer under the cruel oppression by the Whites during the emergency.

While African women are exploited on the basis of race in *The River Between* and *Weep Not, Child*, they are exploited on the basis of class and gender in *A Grain of Wheat*. The sufferings of Thabai women become representative of the sufferings of African women during the Emergency at its peak. Mumbi's suffering as a victim of sexual exploitation is drawn vividly. African women are exploited sexually, both by the white settlers and also by the African homeguards during the Emergency. Economically suppressed African women turn into workers. They are paid low. Thus they are subjected to exploitation on the basis of race, class and gender.

The sexual exploitation of African women which is portrayed in *A Grain of Wheat*, continues in Ngugi's other three novels. The sexual exploitation takes them into three different directions. In *Petals of Blood*, the sexually exploited Wanja takes a negative path in her life as vengeance against the exploitative society and becomes both the exploiter and the exploited. In the *Devil on the Cross*, the protagonist Wariinga in spite of being a victim of sexual exploitation during her school days, takes a positive line and transforms herself into an emancipated educated woman. In *Matigari*, Guthera, a girl of church with high morals, is forced by the prevailing social, economic and political conditions to live a life of a barmaid who trades in flesh. In the later part of the novel, she finds meaning and purpose in her life by revolting against the neo-colonialists and engages herself in the nation-building activity.

Thus Ngugi's aim is to build up the nation, exposing exploitation during the colonial and neo-colonial period. He concentrates on the exploitation of the African women on the basis of race, class and gender. He avoids drawing in detail problems prevalent within the African society such as bride price, polygamy and barrenness as expressed in the novels of African women writers like Buchi Amecheta, Flora Nwapa, Ama Ata Aidoo and Bessie Head. In *Matigari*, Guthera becomes Ngugi's mouthpiece in questioning the rights of women living in an exploited society.

He is not a radical feminist. He is a feminist in a humanistic sense.

In Ngugi's novels, it is not the image but the protest against the messed up change that resulted after colonisation that gains prominence. While Armah's protagonists withdraw themselves and Achebe's characters try to dance the dance of the tribe, Ngugi's characters oppose the changes imposed on them by the white colonisers or the African neo-colonisers. Karega in *Petals of Blood* says:

> Kenyan people had always been ready to resist foreign control and exploitation. The story of this heroic resistance; who will sing it? Their struggles to defend their land, their wealth, their lives; who'll tell it? (236)

Ngugi has portrayed the Kenyan people's struggle in his fictional works. Unlike in Armah or Achebe, Ngugi primarily concerns himself with the nature of exploitation and the protest by the masses. He shows the struggle of the peasants with a much powerful enemy. This reminds one of a novel like *God's Bit of Wood* by Symbene Ousmane. The protagonist in this novel is not a single individual of the suffering mass. In spite of the frustration and disillusion, the struggle goes on. The novelist rightly believes that when the united mass would revolt, no power of exploitation will be able to control it. According to Ngugi,

> Violence in order to change an intolerable, unjust social order is not savagery: it purifies man. Violence to protect and preserve an unjust, oppressive social order is criminal, and diminishes man.[4]

In *The River Between*, Waiyaki, who has a true spirit to lead the people against the cultural exploitation, fails to communicate his wisdom to the people on the ridges at the right time. But 'Kiama' waged a war against the cultural exploitation and also struggled vigorously in getting back the lost lands. In *Weep Not, Child*, Ngotho, who could not brook the unjust practices of the white landlords, particularly in the discrimination in the payment of wages, becomes vociferous and participates in an agitation against the landlord, Howlands. Mau Mau movement, which aims at bringing back to the natives the occupied lands, is drawn as a patriotic movement. Particularly, Jomo Kenyatta, the leader of the movement, Dedan Kimathi who succeeds him after his arrest, and Young Boro, who runs into the forest to fight against the exploitative white government, are portrayed vividly in *Weep Not, Child*.

In *A Grain of Wheat*, Kihika stands for heroic tradition and African cultural heritage. He arouses consciousness in the minds of the people by drawing the colonial brutality into the minds of the people. Like Boro, he fought from the forest. The Mau Mau African warriors are portrayed as patriots who fought for their country in this novel.

In *Petals of Blood*, Karega with his anti neo-colonial attitude inspires the fellow Kenyans and wages a war against the shameless and cruel rulers of Kenya. He covers the length and breadth of Kenya looking for a solution to the problems of the toiling masses of Africa. In *Devil on the Cross*, Wariinga wages a war against the hegemony of dominant neo-colonial culture. In *Matigari*, Matigari comes before us as a rebel who asks questions and creates conditions, which undermine the political system and economic discourse of power.

Ngugi's characters insist on national perspectives on economics, politics and culture. They want a democratic Africa of peasants and workers who can radiate outwards to link with the heroic struggles of other people in other undeveloped countries. For them, the neo-colonial state is the negation of Africa's progress and development. For them, the defeat of imperialism and neo-colonism is of primary concern. They feel that the liberation of natural and human resources and the entire productive forces of the nation would be the beginning of Africa's real progress and development. A Ngugi hero almost tunes with Brecht who addresses the students, workers and peasants of his country thus:

> Your science will be valueless, you will find
> And learning will be sterile, if inviting
> Unless you pledge your intellect to fighting
> against all enemies of mankind.[5]

A Ngugi hero would like to bring about a change in society through violence. In *The River Between*, the conflicts—economic, racial and cultural—remain rather sub-terrain. In other novels, the hero grows and rebels against the conservative, exploitative and selfish custodians of the Kenyan society. Boro in *Weep Not, Child*, Kihika in *A Grain of Wheat*, Karega in *Petals of Blood*, Wariinga in *Devil on the Cross*, Matigari in *Matigari* protest and rebel against exploitation in their societies. They do not hesitate to attack relentlessly 'the corridors' which 'drink human blood' and 'feast on human flesh.'

It is the bane of the European creative artists and historians that they deliberately distorted the African history and maliciously maligned the African heroes. Perhaps their desire for self-glorification made them so. At the hands of writers like Karen Blicxen, Elspeth Huxley, Robert Ruark, Fred Mazdalany, Africa is moved by many serious inadequacies, false touches, flaws and inaccuracies. Perhaps, they have lost their bearings in the maze of African pantheon. They are often apt to flounder or to take safe refuge in comfortable stereotypes in their Africans. In other words, imperfections, bias and personal national prejudices have entered their accounts of Africa. But Ngugi as a writer makes it a point to present a correct picture of Africa.

Ngugi earnestly believes that the story of Africa, particularly of Kenya, has been deliberately distorted by the European writers. So he believes that the past is important as a base for pondering the present and the future. His novels cover the period in Kenyan history dating roughly from the arrival of the Europeans with their religion to Kenya in nineteen twenties to the neo-colonial period till nineteen eighties. They centre on what are among the most momentous events in Kenya's colonial history. They include the earliest coordinated attempt by the Gikuyu people, European colonialism on the political, economic and cultural fronts; the intensification of the nationalist consciousness resulting in the Mau Mau, the aftermath of the war, the victory of independence with its accompanying disappointments. He feels that the African writer has a duty to retell the African story, animate the past and resume the broken dialogue with his people. With his proper sense of history, he has presented a true picture of Africa and this remains his solid achievement to his country.

To conclude, we may say that Ngugi is one writer who is drawn to ever-increasing materialistic outlook and fast-degrading moral values in the society. It is this human aberration reulting in untold misery to the Africans during the British hegemony that has shaken his conscience. He, with his scholastic acumen, has turned to expose vividly this exploitation and all its pernicious ramifications. He expresses that the goal of total liberation can be achieved through the united effort of the peasant, the worker and the student whom he calls the Holy Trinity.

NOTES

1. Edgar Right, *The Critical Evaluation of African Literature* (London: Heinemann, 1973), p. 13.
2. Cheikh Hamidou Kane, *Ambiguous Adventure* (London: James Kerry, 1986), p. 54.
3. Ngugi wa Thiong'o, *Decolonising the Mind* (London: James Kerry, 1987), pp. 29-30.
4. Ngugi wa Thiong'o, "Mau Mau, Violence and Culture," *Homecoming* (London: Heinemann, 1972), p. 28.
5. Brecht, *Collected Poems* (London: Methuen, 1950), p. 450.

Bibliography

NOVELS

Ngugi wa Thiong'o, *Weep Not, Child.* London: Heinemann, 1964.

_____, *The River Between*. London: Heinemann, 1965.

_____, *A Grain of Wheat*. London: Heinemann, 1967.

_____, *Petals of Blood*. London: Heinemann, 1977.

_____, *Devil on the Cross*. London: Heinemann, 1982.

_____, *Matigari*. London: Heinemann, 1986.

SHORT FICTION

Ngugi wa Thiong'o, *Secret Lives*. London: Heinemann, 1975.

PLAYS

_____, *The Black Hermit*. London: Heinemann, 1968.

_____, *This Time Tomorrow*. Nairobi: East African Literature Bureau, 1970.

_____, *The Trial of Dedan Kimathi*. London: Heinemann, 1976. Co-authored with Micere Githae Mugo.

_____, *I Will Marry When I Want*. London: Heinemann, 1982. Co-authored with Ngugi wa Mirii.

NON-FICTION

Ngugi wa Thiong'o, *Homecoming*. London: Heinemann, 1972.

_____, *Detained: A Writer's Prison Dairy*. London: Heinemann, 1981.

_____, *Writers in Politics*. London: Heinemann, 1981.

_____, *Barrel of a Pen: Resistance to Repression in Neo-colonial Kenya*. London: African World Press, 1983.

_____, *Decolonising the Mind: The Politics of Language in African Literature*. London: James Currey, 1986.

_____, *African Literature*. London: James Currey, 1986.

_____, *Writing against Neocolonialism*. London: Vita, 1986.

_____, *Moving the Centre: The Struggle for Cultural Freedom*. London: James Currey, 1993.

ARTICLES

Ngugi wa Thiong'o, "Life in a Village: Memories of Childhood," *The Writer in Modern Africa*, ed. Per Wastberg. Stockholm: African Scandinavian Writers' Conference, (1967), 99-107.

_____, *Satire in Nigeria: Chinua Achebe T.M. Aluko and Wole Soyinka, Protest and Conflict in African Literature*. London: Heinemann, 1969.

_____, "Education for a National Culture," *UFAHAMU*, XII 2 (1983), 20-34.

_____, "The Language of African Literature," *New Left Review*, (1985), 109-27.

INTERVIEWS

Marcuson, Allan, Mike Gonzalez and Dave Williams. "James Ngugi Interviewed by Fellow Students at Leeds University," *CUL*, 31, 1961, p. 2.

Bette J. Parker, BBB Interviews Ngugi wa Thiong'o, *Blacks Books Bulletin*, 6. 1, 1978.

Magina Magina Interviews Ngugi wa Thiong'o. *African Report*, No. 9, February 1979, pp. 30-31.

Martin G. Interviews Ngugi wa Thiong'o. *Kunapipi*, III, 2, 1981.

Eyon Hansel Ndumbe, Interviews Ngugi wa Thiong'o. *Journal of Commonwealth Literature*, 1981, p. 164.

Bjorkman, Ingrid Interviews Ngugi wa Thiong'o, *Kunapipi*, IV, 2 1982.

Amabi, Elechi. Interviews Ngugi wa Thiong'o. *Kunapipi*, V, 1, 1983.

Granqveist, Raoul Interviews Ngugi wa Thiong'o, *Kunapipi*, V, 1, 1983.

OTHER WORKS CONSULTED

NOVELS

Achebe, Chinua. *A Man of the People*. London: Heinemann, 1966.

_____. *Arrow of God*. London: Heinemann, 1966.

_____. *Things Fall Apart*. London: Heinemann, 1958.

_____. *No Longer at Ease*. London: Heinemann, 1963.

Armah, Ayi Kwei. *The Beautyful Ones Are Not Yet Born*. London: Heinemann, 1969.

Conrad, Joseph. *Heart of Darkness*. Bombay: Orient Longman, 1996.

Ekwensi, Cyprian. *Jagua Nana*. London: Heinemann, 1975.

Nazereth, Peter. *The General Is Up*. Calcutta: Writers Workshop, 1984.

Palangyo, Peter K. *Dying in the Sun*. London: Heinemann, 1969.

Soyinka, Wole. *Season of Anomy*. London: Rex Collings, 1973.

POETRY

Walcott, Derek. *The Castaway and Other Poems*. London: Jonathan Cape, 1963.

Whitman, Walt "On the Beach at Night," *American Literature of Nineteenth Century*, William J. Fisher et al. New Delhi: Eurasia, 1964.

NON-FICTIONAL WORKS

Achebe, Chinua. *Morning Yet on Creation Day*. London: Heinemann, 1975.

Bailey Millard, "Rabindranath Tagore Discovers America," *The Book Man*, Vol. 44, No. 1916.

Corinthians. *The Holy Bible*. Book 1, Chapter 15, Line 36.

Kirpal, Viney. "The Third World Fiction," *Recent Commonwealth Literature*. New Delhi: Prestige, 1989.

Narasimhaiah C.D. ed. 'Introduction,' *Commonwealth Literature*. New Delhi: Oxford University Press, 1976.

Sundaram P.S. *R.K. Narayan*. New Delhi: Arnold-Heinemann, 1973.

GENERAL STUDIES ON AFRICAN LITERATURE

BOOKS

Agovi, K.E. *Novels of Social Change*. Tema: Ghana Publishing Corporation, 1988.

Amuta, Chidi. *The Theory of African Literature: Implications for Practical Criticism*. London: Zed, 1989.

Bennett, George. *Kenya: A Political History*. Oxford: Oxford University Press, 1963.

Brett, E.A. *Colonialism and Underdevelopment in East Africa*. London: Heinemann, 1973.

Brown, W. Lloyd. *Women Writers in Africa*. London: Greenwood Press, 1981.

Cartly, Wilfred. *Whispers from a Continent*. London: Heinemann, 1971.

Chinwezu, et al. *Towards the Decolonisation of African Literature*. London: KPI, 1980.

Cook, David. *African Literature: A Critical View*. Harlow: Longman, 1977.

Dathorne, O.R. *African Literature in the Twentieth Century*. Minneapolis: University of Minnesota Press, 1975.

Davidson, Basil. *The People's Cause: A History of Guerrillas in Africa*. London: Longman, 1981.

———. *Africa in Modern History*. Harmondsworth: Penguin, 1978.

Dilly, M. *British Policy in Kenya Colony*. London: Cas, 1966.

Emenyonu, Ernest and C.D. Narasimhaiah, ed. *African Literature Comes of Age*. Mysore: Dhvanyaloka, 1988.

Fanon, Frantz. *The Wretched of the Earth*. Harmondsworth: Penguin, 1967.

Finnegan, Rooth. *Oral Literature in Africa*. Oxford: Oxford University Press, 1980.

Gakwandi, Shatto Arthur. *The Novel and the Contemporary Experience in Africa*. London: Heinemann, 1977.

———. *The Novel: A Contemporary Experience in Africa*. London: Heinemann, 1977.

Gikandi, Simon. *Reading the African Novel*. London: James Currey, 1987.

Gnegeiberger, George M. *Marxism and African Literature*. London: James Currey, 1965

Gowda, Anniah H.H., ed. *The Colonial and Neo-Colonial Encounters in Commonwealth Literature*. Mysore: University of Mysore, 1983.

Inghan, Kenneth. *A History of Africa*. London: Longman, 1965.

Kariuki, J.M. *Mau Mau Detainee*. Oxford: Oxford University Press, 1963.

Kenyatta, Jomo. *Facing Mount Kenya*. Mercury, 1961.

Lambert, H.E. *Kikuyu Social and Political Institutions*. Oxford: Oxford University Press, 1956.

Larson, C.R. *The Emergence of African Fiction*. Bloomington: Indiana University Press, 1972.

Leys, Colin. *Underdevelopment in Kenya*. London: Heinemann, 1975.

Littie Kenneth. *The Sociology of Urban Women's Image in African Literature*. London: Heinemann, 1980.

Mahood, M.M. *The Colonial Encounter*. London: Rex Collings, 1977.

Majdalany, F. *State of Emergency*. London: Longman, 1962.

Mazrui, Ali A. *African Writers on African Writing*, ed. G.D. Killam. London: Heinemann, 1973.

Meyers, Jeffrey. *Fiction and Colonial Experience*. Ipswich: Boydell, 1972.

Moore, Gerald. *Seven African Writers*. London: Oxford University Press, 1962.

_____. *Twelve African Writers*. London: Heinemann, 1980.

Nagara, Emmanuel. *Art and Ideology in the African Novel*. London: Heinemann, 1985.

Nazareth, Peter. *An African View of Literature*. London: Routledge, 1985.

Ogot, B.A and J.A. Kieran. *Zamani: A Survey of East African History*. Nairobi: Longmans of East African Publishing House, 1968.

Oliver R and G. Mathew, ed. *History of East Africa*. Vol. 1, Oxford: Clarendon Press, 1963.

Oliver, Ronald and J.D. Fage. "North-East and East Africa in Medieval and Early Modern Times," *A Short History of Africa*. England: Penguin, 1975.

P'Bitek, Okot. *Africa's Cultural Revolution*. Nairobi: Macmillan Books for Africa, 1973.

Palmer, Eustace. *The Growth of the African Novel*. London: Heinemann, 1979.

Prins, A.H.J. *East African Age-Class Systems*. Westport: Negno Universities Press, 1970.

Tucker, Forres. *Modern Commonwealth Literature*. New York: Frederick Unger, 1977

Wasserman, Garry. *Politics of Decolonisation*. Cambridge: Cambridge University Press, 1967.

Wauthier, Claude. *The Literature and Thought of Modern Africa*. London: Heinemann, 1978.

William, Horosz, *The Crisis of Responsibility: Man as the Source of Accountability*. Horman: University of Oklahoma Press, 1975.

ARTICLES

Comas, James. "The Presence of Theory: Theorizing the Present," *Research in African Literatures*. Vol. 21, No. 1 (Spring 1990), 5-31.

Daimond, Larry. "Fiction as Political Thought," *African Affairs*, Vol. 88, No. 352 (July 1989), 435-45.

Harrow, Kenneth W. "A Formal Approach to African Literature," *Research in African Literatures*, Vol. 21, No. 1 (Spring 1990), 79-89.

Kinyatti, Maina-Wa. "Mau Mau: The Peak of Political Organisation and Struggle for Liberation in Colonial Kenya," *UFAHAMU*, XII, 3 (1983), 90-123.

CRITICAL STUDIES ON NGUGI WA THIONG'O

BOOKS/ANTHOLOGICS

Awoonor, Kofi. "James Ngugi, Ferdinand Oyono and the Anti-Colonial Novel," *The Breast of the Earth*. Enuju: NOK (1975) 281-305.

Baldwin, W. *Mau Mau Manhunt*. New York: E.P. Dutton, 1975.

Barnett, Donald and Karari, Njama. *Mau Mau from Within*. New York: Modern Reader Paperback, 1970.

Cook, David and Okenimkpe, Michael. *Ngugi wa Thiong'o: An Exploration of His Writings*. London: Heinemann, 1983.

Dhar, T.N. "Private Dreams and Public Pressures: Ngugi's *Weep Not, Child* and *The River Between*," *Commonwealth Fiction*, ed. R.K. Dhawan. New Delhi: Classical, 1988. Vol. II, 220-33.

Evans, Jennifer. "Mother Africa and the Heroic Whore: Female Images in *Petals of Blood*," *Contemporary Literature*, ed. Hal Wylie, et al. Washington: Three Continents Press, 1983. 57-65.

Gachukia, Eddah W. "The Novels of James Ngugi," *The Teaching of African Literature in Schools*, ed. Eddah Gachukia and S. Kichamu Akivaga. Nairobi: Kenya Literature Bureau, 1978.

Gachukia, Eddah W. "Chinua Achebe and Tradition," *Standpoints on African Literature: A Critical Anthology*, ed. Chris L.Wanjala. Nairobi, Kampala, Dar es Salaam: East African Literature Bureau, 1973. 172-87.

Gakwandi, Shatto Arthur. *The Novel and Contemporary Experience in Africa*. London: Heinemann, 1977.

Gikandi, Simon. *Reading the African Novel*. London: James Currey, 1987. 149-70.

Indrasena Reddy, K. *The Novels of Achebe and Ngugi: A Study in the Dialectics of Commitment*. New Delhi: Prestige, 1994.

Innes, C.L. *The Devil's Own Mirror*. Washington: Three Continents Press, 1990.

Jones, Eldred D., ed. *African Literature Today*. London: Heinemann, 1972.

Killam, G.D. "Notions of Religion, Alienation and Archetype in *Arrow of God*," *Exile and Tradition: Studies in African and Caribbean Literature*, ed. Rowland Smith. London: Longman, 1976. 152-65.

_____. *An Introduction to the Writing of Ngugi*. London: Heinemann, 1980.

Lindfors, Bernth. "*Petals of Blood* as a Popular Novel," *Contemporary Literature*, ed. Hal Wylie et al. Washington: Three Continents Press, 1983. 49-55.

Manglam Brown, David. *Land, Freedom and Fiction: History and Ideology in Kenya*. London: Zed, 1985.

Moore, Gerald. *The Chosen Tongue*. London: Longman, 1969.

_____. "Chinua Achebe: Nostalgia and Realism," *Twelve African Writers*. London: Hutchinson University Press, 1980.

Mphaheele, Ezekiel. *The African Image*. London: Faber and Faber, 1962.

Ngara, Emmanuel. *Art and Ideology in the African Novel*. London: Heinemann, 1985.

Obiechina, Emmanuel. *Culture, Tradition and Society in the West African Novel*. Cambridge: Cambridge University Press, 1975.

Palmer, Eustace. *An Introduction to the African Novel*. London: Heinemann, 1972.

_____. *The Growth of the African Novel*. London: Heinemann, 1979.

Pieterse, Cosmos and Dennis Duerden. *African Writers Talking*. London: Heinemann, 1973.

Ranga Rao, V. "The Hero in Ngugi wa Thiong'o," *Indian Readings in Commonwealth Literature*, ed. G.S. Amur, et al. New Delhi: Sterling, 1985. 132-36.

Robson, C.B. *Ngugi wa Thiong'o*. London: Macmillan, 1979.

Serumaga, Robert. "A Mirror of Integration: Chinua Achebe and James Ngugi," *Protest and Conflict in African Literature*, ed. Cosmo Pieterse and Donald Munro. New York: African Publishing Corp., 1969. 70-80

Wastberg, Per, ed. *The Writer in Modern Africa*. New York African Publication Corporation, 1969.

Wauthier, C. *The Literature and Thought of Modern Africa*. ed. Shirely Kay. London: Heinemann, 1978.

Were, Gideon S. and Derek A. Wilson. *East Africa through a Thousand Years*. London: Heinemann, 1972.

Zehersten, Arne. "Ngugi wa Thiong'o: The Mubenzi Tribesman," *East African Literature*. London: Longman, 1983. 82-86.

ARTICLES

A special issue on Ngugi wa Thiong'o. *Research in African Literatures*, 16, 2 (Summer 1985).

Aborisade, P.A. "National and Revolutionary Consciousness: Two Phases of Ngugi Artistic Praxis," *UFAHAMU*, XVIII, 2 (1990), 59-74.

Acworth, Will. "Interview with Ngugi wa Thiong'o, *UFAHAMU*, XVIII, 2 (1990), 41-46.

Afejuku, Tony. "Autobiography as History and Political Testament: Ngugi wa Thiong'o's *Detained*," *WLWE*, XXX, 1 (1990), 78-87.

Baloguh, F. "Ngugi's *Petals of Blood*: A Novel of the People," *Bashiru*, X, 2 (n.d.), 49-57.

Baloguh, F. Odun. Ngugi's *Devil on the Cross*: The Novel Hagiography of a Marxist," *UFAHAMU*, XVI, 2 (1988), 76-92.

Berger, Roger A. "Ngugi's Comic Vision," *Research in African Literature*, XX, 1 (1989), 1-25.

Boehmer, Elleke. "The Master's Dance to the Master's Voice: Revolutionary Nationalism and the Representation of Women in the Writing of Ngugi wa Thiong'o," *Journal of Commonwealth Literature*, Vol. 26, 1 (1991), 188-205.

Cochrane, Judith. "Women as Guardians of the Tribe in Ngugi Novels," *ACLALS Bulletin*, IV, 5 (1977), 1-11.

Crehan, Stewart. "The Politics of the Signifier: Ngugi wa Thiong'o's *Petals of Blood*," *WLWE*, XXVI, 1, 1986, 1-24.

Curtis, Lisa. "The Divergence of Art and Ideology in the Later Novels of Ngugi wa Thiong'o: A Critique," *UFAHAMU*, XIII 2-3 (1984), 186-214.

Drame, Kandioura. "Social Function of Myth and Epic: Mongo Beti and Ngugi wa Thiong'o," *UFAHAMU*, XII, 2 (1983), 44-68.

Elders, Derek. "Review of Ngugi's *A Grain of Wheat* in Eldred D. Jones, ed., *African Literature Today*, No. 1. London: Heinemann, 1968.

Eyoh, Hansel Ndumbe. "Ngugi wa Thiong'o," *The Journal of Commonwealth Literature*, XXI, 1 (1986), 162-66.

Gikandi, Simon. "The Epistemology of Translation: Ngugi Matigari, and the Political Language," *RAL*, 22, 1 (Spring 1991).

_____. "On Culture and the State: The Writings of Ngugi wa Thiong'o," *Third World Quarterly*, Vol. 11, No. 1 (Jan. 1989), 148-56.

Glinga, Werner. "*The River Between* and its Forerunners: A Contribution to the Theory of the Kenyan Novel." *WLWV*, XXVI, 2, 1986, 211-28.

Goodwin, K.L. "Nationality-Chauvinism Must Burn. Utopian Vision in *Petals of Blood* and *Matigari*," *The Literary Criterion*, XXVII, 3 (1991), 1-14.

Gordimer, Nadine. "A Tyranny of Clowns," *New York Times Book Review*, 21 (February 1988), 1 & 26.

Harrow, Kenneth. "Ngugi wa Thiong'o's *A Grain of Wheat*: Season of Irony," *Research in African Literatures*, XVI, 2 (1985), 243-63.

Ikiddeh, Ime. "James Ngugi as Novelist," *African Literature Today*, 2 (1969), 3-10.

Inderasena Reddy, K. "Optimism in Ngugi's *Petals of Blood*," *Kakatiya Journal of English Studies*, 8 (1987-88), 134-43.

Jabbi, Bu-Buakei. "Conrad's Influence on Betrayal in *A Grain of Wheat*," *Research in African Literatures*, XI (Spring 1980), 50-83.

_____. "The Structure of Symbolism in *A Grain of Wheat*," *Research in African Literatures*, XVI, 2 (1985), 210-42.

Kirsten, Holst Peterson. "Birth Pangs of a Consciousness Mau Mau and Ngugi wa Thiong'o," *WLWE*, XX, 2, 1981, 214-27.

Kozain, Rustom. "Form as Politics, or the Tyranny of Narrativity. Re-reading Ngugi wa Thiong'o's *Petals of Blood*," *UFAHAMU*, XVIII, 3 (1990), 77-90.

Maughan-Brown, David. "Four Sons of One Father: A Comparison of Ngugi's Earliest Novels with Work by Mwangi Mangua, and Wachira," *Research in African Literatures*, XVI, 2 (1985), 179-209.

Ngau, Margaret. "Women's Participation in Education and National Development: The Dilemma of Institutional Bias in Kenya." *UFAHAMU*, XVI, 2 (1988), 3-19.

Nwankwo, Chimalum. "Shifting the Grain from the Husk: An Overview of Ngugi's Writing," *The Literary Half-Yearly*, XXV, 1 (1984), 2-15.

Nwahunanya, Chinyee. "The Outsider in West African Fiction," *The Literary Half-Yearly*, XXX, 1 (1989).

Nwankwo, Chimalum. "Women in Ngugi's Plays: From Passivity to Social Responsibility," *UFAHAMU*, XIV, 3 (1985), 85-92.

Nwankwo, Chimalum. "Uhurusa! Freedom Now!" *KUNAPIPI*, XVI, 2, 1982, 123-38.

Pagnoulle, Christine. "Ngugi wa Thiong'o's *Journey of the Magi*: Part 2 of *Petals of Blood*," *Research in African Literatures*, XVI, 2 (1985), 264-75.

Palmer, E. "Ngugi's *Petals of Blood*," *ALT*, 10 (1979), 153-66.

Panduranga Rao, V. "A Critique on the Hero in Ngugi's *Petals of Blood*," *African Literature Today*. New Delhi: Prestige, 1964.

Porter, Abioseh M. "Ideology and the Image of Women: Kenyan Women in Njau and Ngugi," *RAL*, XII, 3 (July 1981), 61-74.

Reed, John. "James Ngugi and the African Novel," *The Journal of Commonwealth Literature*, 1, London: Heinemann, 1965.

_____. "James Ngugi and the African Novel," *JCL*, I, 2 (1965), 117-21.

_____. "Ngugi's New Strength," A Review of *A Grain of Wheat*. *JCL*, 5 (July 1968), 135-36.

Sharma, Govind Narain. "Ngugi's *Detained* as a Modern Consolation," *Research in African Literatures*, XIX, 4 (1988), 520-28.

_____. "Socialism and Civilization: The Revolutionary Traditionalism of Ngugi wa Thiong'o," *ARIEL*, XIX, 2 (1988), 21-30.

_____. "Ngugi's Christian Vision: Theme and Pattern in *A Grain of Wheat*," *African Literature Today*, 10 (1979), 167-76.

_____. "Ngugi's Apocalypse: Marxism, Christianity and African Utopianism in *Petal of Blood*," *WLWE*, XVIII, 2 (1979), 302-13.

Sicherman, Carol M. "Ngugi wa Thiong'o and the Writing of Kenyan History," *Research in African Literatures*, XX, 3 (1989), 347-70

Sivaramakrishna, V. "James Ngugi," *Triveni*, Vol. 55, No. 1 (1986), 28-37.

Williams, Katherine. "Decolonising the World: Language, Culture and Self in the Works of Ngugi wa Thiong'o and Gabriel Okara." *RAL*, 22, 4, 1991.

Williams, Lloyd. "Religion and Life in James Ngugi's *The River Between*," *African Literature Today*, 5 (1971), 54-65.

Zehersten, Arne. "Ngugi wa Thiong'o: The Mubenzi Tribesman," *East African Literature*. London: Longman (1983), 82-86.

List of Abbreviations

WNC	*Weep Not, Child*
RB	*The River Between*
GW	*A Grain of Wheat*
PB	*Petals of Blood*
DC	*Devil on the Cross*
Mg	*Matigari*